Praise for *Leadership and Self-Deception*

"This is a profound book with deep and sweeping implications. I couldn't recommend it more highly."

—**Stephen R. Covey, author of *The 7 Habits of Highly Effective People***

"This is the most profound and practical business book I have ever read! Everyone I have recommended this book to has been challenged intellectually and also touched emotionally. It is a must-read that I will give to my kids to read before they begin their careers."

—**Tom A. DiDonato, Senior Vice President, Human Resources, Lear Corporation**

"I love this book. It identifies the central issue in all organizational performance. Like truth itself, this book reveals more with each re-examination. I highly recommend it."

—**Doug Hauth, Business Development Manager, Convio, Inc.**

"It's rare to find a business book that is good enough to recommend to your boss, your work team, and your friends. The concepts in this book have transformed both the way I work and the way I live."

—**Robert W. Edwards, Managing Director, Sales, FedEx**

"This astonishing book is a *must*-read for every executive or personal and professional coach."

—**Laura Whitworth, coauthor of *Co-Active Coaching* and cofounder, The Coaches Training Institute**

"After decades of executive leadership in senior management positions, I've finally found in Arbinger what I consider to be the best means of improving every measure of success. From boosting the bottom line to increasing personal joy, this book shows the way."

—**Bruce L. Christensen, former President and CEO, PBS**

T0191363

"The leadership principles in this book have had a greater impact on the quality of leadership in our company than anything we have ever implemented. They have been extraordinarily important in helping make our company a great place to work while at the same time helping us focus on results and increase productivity as never before."

—Michael Stapley, President and CEO, DMBA

"Simple...clear...powerful. With many years of experience in leadership, organizational development, and training, I was surprised to find something strike me with such impact."

—Janet Steinwedel. President, Leader's Insight

"Are you relating to the world anxiously or angrily, not comprehending why you hold judgmental attitudes, feel uncontrollable fear, or unleash explosions of temper against your colleagues without being able to explain why? Do you feel hopeless and unable to change? Learn the practical tools provided in this fascinating book and eliminate this problem at its source right now!"

—Marcos Cajina Heinzkill, Certified Coach and Facilitator, founder and President, Renewal, Spain

"This book is a rare gem that is treasured by all who have read it. The organization for which I work has passed this book to so many people, and it is amazing to watch people's attitudes and behaviors toward each other changing. Each day everyone gives a little more, making us better leaders, but more importantly, better people."

—Nuala Murphy, Senior Vice President, global financial services company

"I've been in the book publishing business for twenty-five years. Rarely have I read a book as profound and life-changing as *Leadership and Self-Deception*."

—David Sanford, Literary Agent, Credo Communications

"This book was recommended to me at an annual strategic planning session. I was stunned by the truth of it and the simple solution. Our entire management has now read it. It has been a building block for our personal and organizational development."

—**Rick Chalk, CEO, Cal-Tex Protective Coatings**

"My business partners and I built a healthcare company on the ideas in this book. We are amazed at what it has helped us achieve. Careful reading and rereading of this book has proven better than any productivity, team-building, or leadership training we've encountered."

—**Mark Ballif, CEO, Plum Healthcare**

"The concepts in this book are powerful. They are fundamental to success whether on the playing field, in the office, or perhaps most importantly, at home. Read this book and you'll see what I mean."

—**Steve Young, two-time NFL Most Valuable Player**

"Rarely has a book had such an immediate and profound impact on the hundreds of CEOs of fast-growth firms we work with through our MIT/Inc./EO Executive Program. And it's one of those rare books that touches both the personal as well as professional lives of these leaders."

—**Verne Harnish, cofounder, Entrepreneurs' Organization, and CEO, Gazelles, Inc.**

"Remarkable. Arbinger possesses the hidden key to productivity and creativity. Do whatever you can to get your hands on this material."

—**Dave Browne, former President and CEO, LensCrafters**

"*Leadership and Self-Deception* is a touchstone for authentic leadership. Arbinger's innovative exploration of what lies beneath behavior uplifts, enlightens, and transforms. We've wholeheartedly adopted *Leadership and Self-Deception* as the foundational material for our administrator development program."

—**Troy S. Buer, Educational Program Director, University of Virginia School of Medicine**

"This is probably the most outstanding book that directs us to soul-searching and introspection. It teaches us to take accountability for our lives and our destinies in a down-to-earth and bluntly practical manner. The lessons in this book have helped me personally, as well as other people I love."

—Kalyan Banerjee, cofounder and Senior Vice President, MindTree

"The principles of *Leadership and Self-Deception* provide the groundwork for our success as individuals and organizations. I recommend it highly to my fellow board members and to global networks, corporate clients, entrepreneurs, and individuals alike."

—Heidi Forbes Öste, CEO and founder, 2BalanceU, and Public Relations, Europe Region, Business and Professional Women International

"While reading, I reviewed my life, and, sure enough, any successes were based on Arbinger's principles. This book is a tool that could transform and elevate the way government functions!"

—Mark W. Cannon, former Administrative Assistant to the Chief Justice of the United States and Staff Director, Commission on the Bicentennial of the US Constitution

"Imagine working in an organization where the aim of your colleagues is to help you achieve your results. I could not believe it possible. After reading this book I just had to bring Arbinger to the UK to teach our people. What an experience! We are all better people for it. This book touches the very foundation of culture, teamwork, and performance."

—Mark Ashworth, President and CEO, Butcher's Pet Care, UK

LEADERSHIP AND SELF-DECEPTION

The Outward Mindset
How to Change Lives and Transform Organizations

The Anatomy of Peace
Resolving the Heart of Conflict

LEADERSHIP AND SELF-DECEPTION

The Secret to Transforming Relationships & Unleashing Results

Revised and Updated Fourth Edition

THE ARBINGER INSTITUTE

Berrett–Koehler Publishers, Inc.

Berrett-Koehler Publishers, Inc.
1333 Broadway, Suite 1000
Oakland, CA 94612-1921
Tel: (510) 817-2277, Fax: (510) 817-2278
www.bkconnection.com

Ordering information

Quantity sales. Special discounts are available on quantity purchases by corporations, associations, and others. For details, contact the "Special Sales Department" at the Berrett-Koehler address above.

Individual sales. Berrett-Koehler publications are available through most bookstores. They can also be ordered directly from Berrett-Koehler: Tel: (800) 929-2929; Fax: (802) 864-7626; www.bkconnection.com

Orders for college textbook/course adoption use. Please contact Berrett-Koehler: Tel: (800) 929-2929; Fax: (802) 864-7626.

Distributed to the U.S. trade and in Publisher Services.

Berrett-Koehler and the BK logo are registered trademarks of Berrett-Koehler Publishers, Inc.

Printed in Canada

Berrett-Koehler books are printed on long-lasting acid-free paper. When it is available, we choose paper that has been manufactured by environmentally responsible processes. These may include using trees grown in sustainable forests, incorporating recycled paper, miniizing chlorine in bleaching, or recycling the energy produced at the paper mill.

Library of Congress Cataloging-in-Publication Data

Names: Arbinger Institute, issuing body.
Title: Leadership and Self-Deception : The Secret to Transforming
   Relationships & Unleashing Results / The Arbinger Institute
Description: Fourth edition. | Oakland, CA : Berrett-Koehler
   Publisher, Inc., [2024] | Includes index.
Identifiers: LCCN 2024007271 (print) | LCCN 2024007272 (ebook) |
   ISBN 9781523006564 (paperback) | ISBN 9781523006571 (pdf) |
   ISBN 9781523006588 (epub)
Subjects: LCSH: Leadership. | Self-deception.
Classification: LCC HD57.7 .L4315 2024 (print) | LCC HD57.7
   (ebook) | DDC 658.4/092—dc23/eng/20240402
LC record available at https://lccn.loc.gov/2024007271
LC ebook record available at https://lccn.loc.gov/2024007272

Fourth Edition

32 31 30 29 28 27 26 24 24   10 9 8 7 6 5 4 3 2 1

Copyediting and proofreading: PeopleSpeak
Interior illustrations and cover design: Michael Brown

"It is in the darkness of their eyes that men get lost."

BLACK ELK

CONTENTS

A NOTE REGARDING THE FOURTH EDITION

The book in your hands includes important changes and incorporates new characters that have not appeared in previous editions of *Leadership and Self-Deception*.

As an institute, we are constantly seeking to expand, refine, and better articulate our message. While the core ideas at the heart of this book remain the same, we have endeavored to present them in a way that is even more accessible and immediately applicable for a wider audience.

If you are a returning reader, we hope you find this new edition both familiar and refreshing. If you are reading this book for the first time, we hope it helps you in the challenges you may be facing in both the workplace and your personal life.

PREFACE

The problem of self-deception is both urgent and universal. In professional and private settings alike, the recurring challenges we face in our relationships and organizations stem from—or are made worse by—our failure to see ourselves and others clearly: as people. Each of us exists in relationship. Some connections bring joy, while others fuel frustration and pain. But it is regrettably common—and frighteningly easy—to lose sight of the humanity of others.

As an institute, our mission is to bring humanity to the workplace. Our clients have achieved remarkable results by applying the ideas you will encounter in this book to bring humanity to their work. Their experiences have repeatedly confirmed how seeing others clearly is foundational to personal and organizational success.

The story that unfolds in this book mirrors how individuals learn and apply these ideas inside our client organizations every day to transform relationships and unleash organizational results. Using a fictional narrative has allowed us to gather, combine, and adapt a wide variety of real-life stories and experiences that are woven into the story in these pages.

This book is about learning to understand, recognize, and mitigate self-deception. It is about learning to see other people and ourselves clearly. We hope it helps you live and lead in a way that is grounded in the foundational truth that *others matter like we matter*.

PART I

A DISEASE OF PERCEPTION

1 • THE CALLOUT

"You have a problem," Theo said. The lines of his face, so recently animated with laughter, now lay still. "And it's a problem we have to address if you two are going to make it here at Zagrum."

The words were met by stunned silence from the room's other occupants, Ana Rivera and Tom Callum. They had both heard about the two-day, closed-door orientation led by Theodore Jefferson for new leaders at Zagrum, but neither of them had anticipated it going like this.

Panic flitted across Tom's face, replaced almost instantly by a guarded, wary look. His mind raced back four months to the day he'd been laid off from his previous company, and his hands clenched the armrests of his chair.

Across the table, Ana had taken a short, involuntary breath. Her face went pale, and her brown eyes flickered from Theo's wire-rimmed glasses to Tom's closed expression. She'd been afraid something like this would happen.

Ana opened her mouth to respond, but Tom cut her off. "What do you mean, Theo? We've only been here a month."

Stifling her annoyance, Ana quickly added, "Of course, we're still working out the kinks with all the merger details. And figuring out how to best coordinate our teams has been a bit..." She glanced again at Tom's scowl. "Challenging." *To put it mildly,* she thought.

"The problem is bigger than the merger," Theo replied, his deep voice gentle. "And a month has been plenty of time to see it." He didn't enjoy provoking discomfort, but he had to get their attention.

"You are Zagrum's newest leaders," Theo continued, "and you're joining us at a busy time for the company. I know you're still getting the lay of the land and that your teams need you. But facing this problem is more important." Theo looked at Ana. "It's more important than Tom's implementation timeline, as crucial as that is for our new product line to succeed. And," he said, turning to Tom, "it's more important than hitting the ambitious sales numbers Ana's team has established, as much as we need to turn over inventory and reach our revenue targets."

"All right," Tom said brusquely, trying to cover his nerves and look proactive. "Let's get to it then. What's the issue here? Tell us what we need to do differently."

Theo laughed, a quick thunderclap of sound. "I wish it were that simple."

The frown on Tom's face deepened.

"This problem doesn't have an easy fix," Theo continued. "It's at the root of all organizational dysfunction. It undermines leadership, stifles innovation, and gets in the way of real collaboration. But despite the issues it causes, the problem is often overlooked and almost always misunderstood. Acting differently isn't enough to solve it."

Ana's brow furrowed. "I don't understand, Theo."

"That's okay," he replied simply. "The problem we're here to address is called *self-deception*, and twenty years ago it nearly tore Zagrum apart. Lou Herbert was the CEO at the time, and he and his team barely managed to turn things around. Since then, understanding and mitigating self-deception has been a key strategic priority for the company."

"So what is it?" Ana asked, keeping her voice level but internally bracing for the worst.

"And how do you know it's an issue for us?" Tom said, his arms folded.

Theo acknowledged Ana's question with a nod, then met Tom's gaze. "Because," he said, smiling, "I have the same problem."

2 · THE DEEPER PROBLEM

"Early on in my career as an attorney," Theo began, "I joined a law firm in Boston and was assigned to work on a major financing project involving thirty banks around the world. Our client was the lead lender on the deal, and I was thrilled to be involved."

Theo smiled, remembering. "It had all the things I'd dreamed about during the long grind of law school: international travel, intricate legal issues, the chance to network with high-profile people, and dollar amounts with more zeros than I'd ever seen. I was the second-most-junior member of the team, and my job was to draft the fifty or so agreements that sat underneath the major lending contract. It was a heavy load of tedious work, but I was eager to prove myself.

"Just one week after I'd been assigned to the project, Tracie and I found out she was pregnant with our first child. Between my work and our baby preparations, the next eight months flew by. On December 22, our son David was born. We couldn't have been more nervous or more excited."

The memory shone in Theo's eyes. He looked from Ana to Tom. "Do either of you have kids?"

Ana smiled. "I have a nine-year-old daughter named Miranda and a six-year-old son, Mateo."

Tom cleared his throat as Theo looked at him. "Yeah, my daughter, Rebecca. She's almost sixteen."

"It changes everything, doesn't it?" Theo leaned forward. "Like the world has a new center of gravity.

"Anyway, I worked hard to wrap up or trade off my assignments so that I could take three weeks off when David was born. We were exhausted and we were happy.

"But then came the phone call. It was December 29. The lead partner on the deal wanted everyone in San Francisco at the client's offices, ASAP. Some details had shifted in a way that dramatically shortened our timeline, and it was all hands on deck.

"'How long?'" I asked.

"'We're here until the deal closes—could be three weeks, could be three months.'

"I was crushed to leave Tracie and our week-old baby. And I felt robbed of the extra time off I had earned."

Ana made a sympathetic noise.

"It took me two days to get ready to leave. If Tracie's sister hadn't volunteered to help out, I'm not sure what we would have done.

"When I arrived, I discovered that I was the last one on the scene, and I got razzed for being late to the party. No one asked about our baby. The only remaining guest office was on the twenty-first floor. The deal headquarters, and everyone else, was on the twenty-fifth. So I hunkered down and got to work, barely noticing the start of the new year. From six in the morning until after midnight each day, I tried to finalize the various details of the legal agreements. Two or three times a day I would go down to the deli in the lobby and buy an overpriced and underwhelming sandwich or salad. Then I'd eat while poring over the documents. I felt alone on the twenty-first floor, isolated with my work and my photos from home.

"I called Tracie most afternoons. Between student debt, the cost of living in Boston, and the baby expenses, we were pretty cash-strapped. Plus, long-distance calls were expensive back then, so the phone calls were short. They left me longing for home and feeling more bitter about the project."

Tom was listening to the story with his arms folded across his chest, his mouth a straight line. Ana's head was slightly tilted, concern on her face.

"If you had asked me at the time what my work objective was, I would have probably said, 'Drafting the best possible documents to protect our client and close the deal,' or something like that. I was clearly committed, right?"

Ana nodded, and Tom shrugged agreement.

"But you should know a couple of other things about this experience. All of the key negotiations were happening on the twenty-fifth floor. They should have been very important to me." Theo tapped on the table to punctuate each word he said next. "Every single change to the deal made on the twenty-fifth floor had to be accounted for in the documents I was drafting.

"But I didn't go up to twenty-five much. In fact, it wasn't until after ten days of lackluster deli food that I noticed there was round-the-clock catering on the twenty-fifth floor for everyone working on the deal."

Ana winced.

"That sure would've been nice to know, right?" Theo said. "I got chewed out on two occasions for not including some of the latest adjustments in my documents, even though plenty of people could have mentioned them to me. On top of that, someone complained about me being hard to find—like it was my fault I got the worst office."

Tom settled his chin against his fist, elbow on the conference table.

"Let me ask you both," Theo said, "just from what you now know about my San Francisco experience, would you say that I was really committed to 'drafting the best possible documents to protect our client and close the deal'?"

"No," Tom answered without hesitation. "You were preoccupied with missing your family and how you weren't being included, so your focus wasn't actually on the result."

"Well, that doesn't seem entirely fair," Ana objected. "Your boss pulled you in to work during your time off, and you probably should've had parental leave to begin with."

"Valid points," Theo said. "And later, when I left that firm, it was mostly because I needed to find a better work-life balance. But Tom is also right," Theo continued. "I wasn't fully engaged.

"When I joined the firm, I knew I was signing up for long hours and inconvenient travel. But here—when we most needed the project to come together—my frustration and resentment were keeping me from offering my best work. I wasn't thinking about our client, my coworkers, or any of the other people impacted by the way I was doing my job."

Tom was nodding. Ana looked unconvinced.

"But how do you think I would have reacted if anyone had told me I seemed distracted, or uncommitted, or disengaged?" Theo asked.

Tom grunted, "Not well. People hate being called out."

"I'm sure I would have gotten defensive," Theo replied. "And I had plenty of excuses! After all, who left behind a new baby? I did. Who was working eighteen-to-twenty-hour days? I was." His voice started to rise. "Who was essentially exiled to work four floors beneath everyone else? Me. And who got left out of basic details like food plans and contract changes? All me.

"As far as I knew, no one else had the challenges I did, but I was working hard despite them. In fact, in my mind, I might've been the most committed and engaged person on the deal! But any member of my team could have told you I had a problem," Theo continued, "a problem with my focus, my engagement, and even my performance. I was failing to catch issues I was hired to anticipate, and it was negatively impacting our project at a critical moment.

"But I had an even deeper problem," Theo said. "Any guesses?"

Tom and Ana glanced at each other, but neither spoke.

Theo leaned forward. "The bigger problem was that I couldn't *see* I had a problem."

3 • STUCK

"I was stuck," Theo continued. "I wasn't telling myself the truth about what was going on, and my view of others had become distorted. I was self-deceived."

Tom made a skeptical noise and leaned back into his chair, remembering how Theo had claimed they all had the same problem.

Theo either didn't notice or didn't mind. "Even though the term sounds theoretical or philosophical, self-deception isn't an academic issue. It's at the heart of the people problems we grapple with every single day. It helps explain how and why we sometimes cause or amplify our own challenges but seem to be completely unaware that we are doing so.

"But before I get ahead of myself, what do you think? How could I be utterly convinced I was dedicated and self-sacrificing in San Francisco when everyone else on the project could see that I was distracted and disengaged?"

Ana spoke up. "Well, it's not like you didn't have any valid reasons to be distracted or even resentful, right?"

"I certainly felt justified."

Ana's brow furrowed. "It sounds like you're saying that the circumstances didn't matter, like you should've been able to perform at your best despite the conditions or how you were treated. But people aren't robots, right? Isn't it illogical to expect your work to be unaffected by your situation?"

"It's a fair point, Ana. Employee well-being and productivity are impacted by many different factors, some of which are simply outside of an individual's control. I didn't choose that project deadline, and it wasn't my fault that everyone couldn't fit comfortably on the same floor."

Ana nodded.

"But there were things I could have done differently," Theo continued. "Instead of isolating myself and indulging in my self-pity, I could have reached out to the people it was my job to coordinate and collaborate with. I can't have been the only one having a challenging time, and I certainly wasn't the only one who was working hard. And just think of how much sooner I could have learned about the catering if I had gone upstairs where the teamwork was happening!

"I wasn't seeing things clearly. I was focused on myself and making excuses. Those are all symptoms of what we're talking about—self-deception. And there's no way to begin to change if you can't see the problem.

"Here's what I'd like you to do," Theo said, looking from Ana to Tom. "It's been about a month since we hired you, Tom, and about a month since the merger brought you to us, Ana. I think that's been enough for you to see this issue at play here at Zagrum. Take a minute to think about where you're seeing this happen. Are you running into people who are self-focused, disengaged, or causing issues that they seem to be unaware of? Have you experienced any of this on your teams? Write down what you've noticed."

Ana uncapped her pen and pulled out a notebook. In the center of the table was a small stack of company-branded notepads and Theo slid one over to Tom.

Both Tom and Ana wrote slowly at first and then picked up steam.

"Okay," Theo said after a few minutes had passed. "Let's hear what you've got. Why don't we start with you, Tom?"

"Oh, I didn't realize we'd be asked to share," Tom said, then cleared his throat. "I've been impressed with everyone here, for the most part. It's a great company."

"But that's not what you wrote down," Theo said, smiling.

"Right. Well, to be honest, I've been hearing about problems being caused by the sales team."

Ana's posture stiffened. Tom didn't seem to notice. "I know this isn't the first time you've heard this, Ana. My team says there's more than one sales rep who keeps promising a deliverable or pricing that's out of touch with reality. And I hear they get pretty wound up when we try to set them straight."

Ana glanced at Theo, torn between the need to defend her team and the awkwardness of arguing in front of a senior executive.

"Don't you think that's an oversimplification, Tom?" Her voice was strained.

Tom waved a dismissive hand. "We've already talked about this. Your people are so eager to close a deal that they don't consider realistic timelines or restraints, and then they expect us to somehow make it all happen."

"I know your product team doesn't like feeling rushed," Ana said, "but if we don't capitalize on the momentum of this new product line, our sales will tank."

"Everything is going to tank anyway if we keep offering people custom features that we can't support."

"That was one single deal for a special client that I personally—"

"Okay!" Theo's booming laughter filled the room. "Things are getting interesting!"

Tom's face closed, and Ana looked down at the table as they both realized they were arguing in front of Theodore Jefferson.

"Sounds like you two have had this conversation before," Theo said with an unfazed grin. "How's it been working out?"

Tom grunted.

"This might surprise you," Theo continued, "but I've been in a fair share of conflicts over the years. And you know what? Blame and defensiveness never seem to get me where I'd like to go."

"I'm sorry," Ana murmured.

"Oh, I'm not looking for an apology!" Theo responded. "This is exactly what we're here for."

To verbally duke it out? Tom thought.

"It's my job to help you become the kind of leaders who invite collaboration and unlock the potential of others," Theo continued. "And, if there are problems, to help you work through them and get unstuck. But, unfortunately, there's no leadership tactic, communication technique, or secret formula that will make any real difference in solving this issue between your teams, or in your ultimate success for that matter."

"Come again?" Tom asked.

Theo grinned. "What I mean is that there's no behavior you can engage in as a leader that will make any lasting difference *unless* you see yourself and the people you impact clearly. If you're going to be successful leaders, the first and most important step is learning how to see."

4 • THE WORK OF A LEADER

"What does it mean to be a leader?" Theo asked. "To you personally?"

Ana thought for a moment. "To support others as they do their job."

"Good," Theo said. "Tom?"

"Being a leader means organizing and directing the work of a team."

Theo stood up and wrote their answers on a large whiteboard. "Anything else?"

"Making sure people are doing what they're supposed to be doing," Tom added.

"And gathering input and motivating others to get results," Ana said.

"Good," Theo said. "So what gets in the way of doing all this? Why isn't it simple to motivate people or direct a team? What makes it hard to get results?"

"Well, we're dealing with people," Ana said. "There's no one-size-fits-all approach that will work with every personality or circumstance. It's not always clear what the best course of action is."

"What else?" Theo asked.

"Some people are just incompetent or lazy," Tom said. "I've met plenty of people who don't take pride in their work or who hate being told what to do."

"All right," Theo said, finishing the notes he was taking on the board.

"I want to take a minute and clarify a few things. You're not here at Zagrum because of your credentials or references, as impressive as they are. You're not even here solely based on your ability to get results. You're here to lead. That means more than having a title or giving orders. We view leadership as the responsibility and opportunity to facilitate the growth and success of others."

Ana wrote in her notebook, wanting Theo to see she was taking the training seriously.

"But your ability to lead well depends on whether or not you see clearly," Theo continued. "Accurate perception is foundational to effective leadership."

"You mean accurate perception like seeing the big picture?" Ana asked. "Or do you mean anticipating problems before they happen?"

"Both are important. But I mean something even more foundational. I'm talking about accurate perception in the way we see ourselves and others. The most important work of a leader is to see clearly and to help others see clearly too.

"See what exactly?" Tom asked.

"That others are people like we are, who matter like we do."

"Isn't that obvious?" Tom sounded unimpressed.

"You'd think so," Theo said. "But when it comes to human interaction, things can get convoluted. Self-deception distorts how we see and engage with each other, and it blinds us to the ways we invite dysfunction in our relationships."

Ana was writing what Theo was saying, but Tom was clearly skeptical.

"Let me ask you this, Tom," Theo said. "Have you ever tried to teach someone something, or persuade them to change, and failed?"

"Of course!" Tom said. "I have a teenage daughter, remember?"

"Any examples you'd be willing to share?" Theo asked.

Tom thought for a moment. "Yeah. Becca's shoes come untied because she ties them wrong. I've tried to show her how to make the loops a square knot—because it holds better and takes the exact same amount of time—but she just gets mad and blows me off."

"I'm assuming Rebecca's problem isn't that she doesn't notice her laces come untied," Theo noted.

"Of course not. She complains about it every time we go running."

"The two of you go running together?"

"It's about the only thing she's willing to do with me consistently, so I'll take it."

"I love it!" Theo said. "But she's not changing the way she ties her shoes in a way that you think would solve the problem."

"Nope. She just gets mad at me anytime I bring it up."

"So how are you seeing the problem here, Tom?" Theo asked.

"I mean, it's not rocket science. The problem is that she won't tie her shoes right. She's too stubborn to listen to me or too lazy to spend one minute learning something that would save her time and frustration."

Tom shook his head, agitated. Ana had a faint frown on her face as she watched the exchange.

"Perfect example," Theo said. "You can see the change Rebecca should make and why it would be better for her if she did, but she resists. And the resistance seems baffling."

"I'm sure that if someone else told her the exact same thing, she'd listen." Tom sounded exasperated. "But I'm her dad."

"So maybe there's some resistance toward *you*, not just the information," Theo said. "Can I ask you another question?"

Tom barked out a short laugh. "I didn't mean to get into my home life, and I don't know what else there is to say, but fire away."

"How are you seeing Rebecca in this situation?"

"What do you mean?"

"I heard you say that she's too stubborn to learn from you or too lazy to give it the time."

"She can be that way, yeah." Tom nodded.

"Okay. And you think she'd probably listen if you weren't her dad. How do you think she's seeing you?" Theo asked.

Tom thought about the last time he'd brought up the shoelace thing and how his daughter had rolled her eyes and said, "You're such a control freak, Dad."

"Well," Tom said, "she probably thinks I'm controlling, maybe too opinionated or critical."

"Okay," Theo said. "Thanks for sharing. So you see her as stubborn; she sees you as controlling. When we're in conflict, we often see each other in negative ways that are mutually reinforcing. That's exactly what I meant when I said that self-deception distorts how we see each other. It's easy to start seeing those around us as problems or obstacles. And that happens between individuals and between groups of people too.

"In fact," Theo said, looking at both Tom and Ana now, "it's pretty clear this is the same dynamic that is at play between your teams. Ana, how does your sales team see Tom's people on the product side?"

"Well…" She shifted in her chair, weighing how frank she should be. "I think they're frustrated. Product doesn't seem open to the feedback we gather from customers, even though it would help us create better products. We make requests and only get a bunch of jargon back, basically some variation of 'It's too late to make any changes.' And that's if we get a response at all."

Tom's jaw tightened as Theo wrote on the whiteboard, "Sales sees Product as unhelpful, closed to feedback, and unresponsive."

"What about you, Tom?" Theo asked. "How has Product been seeing Sales?"

"First of all, we've made several adjustments based on customer feedback, but everyone wants some kind of magic product that doesn't cost anything to make and is ready to ship out yesterday. And if my engineers had to immediately respond to every rep's email about a product tweak or expedited process, they'd never have time to do their jobs. But since my team isn't pocketing any commission, our focus is on quality."

"That's not really fair," Ana replied.

Tom shrugged, "That's just what I'm hearing from my team."

"Okay," Theo cut in. "Here's what I'm hearing." He spoke the words as he wrote them: "Product sees Sales as impatient, unrealistic, greedy."

"Here's a snapshot of how your teams are seeing one another." Theo looked at the board and whistled. "And doesn't this look like the perfect recipe for thriving collaboration!"

HOW SALES SEES PRODUCT	HOW PRODUCT SEES SALES
· Unhelpful	· Impatient
· Closed to feedback	· Unrealistic
	· Greedy
· Unresponsive	

His tone was light, but his eyes were serious. "We could spend these next two days assigning blame and finding fault. And ultimately, it wouldn't get us anywhere. The real problem is much deeper than behavior—deeper than making unrealistic promises to customers or being slow to answer emails. The real problem is this." He tapped the board. "The way your teams are *seeing* each other, and the fact that each of them believes that their perception is the truth. The perception your teams have of each other shapes every interaction between Product and Sales."

"But the perception didn't come out of nowhere," Tom said. "And some things are objectively true. I've looked over the changes we've made from customer feedback, and I can show you the mountain of emails from Sales."

"You think I don't have any evidence from my team?" Ana arched an eyebrow. "I can look up exactly how many contracts we've lost by not being more responsive to fairly minor customer requests."

"Hold on," Theo said. "That's not the point. The point is that we've got two teams who are both convinced the other is completely at fault. And because each side believes the other is to blame, both feel powerless to fix the issues. It's causing frustration, distrust, and inefficiency. Something obviously needs to change. So where do we start?"

Neither Tom nor Ana spoke.

"From where I'm sitting," Theo said, "you both have a choice to make. It looks like your teams have recruited you into their way of seeing things. You can double down and keep taking sides, or you can lead your teams to solve the real problem."

"Sounds pretty straightforward when you put it like that," Ana said.

"I'd be the first to admit that it can be tempting to pick sides as a leader," Theo said. "It's normal to feel more sympathetic toward your own team. And few things can unify a group so quickly as facing a common enemy.

"But we can't afford to be enemies here. When teams can't figure out how to work together, companies die. It's the same for any relationship, no matter where the conflict started or how objectively right a person feels their viewpoint is."

Tom and Ana were avoiding each other's eyes.

"If we can't see the real problem, we can't solve it. In fact," Theo said, "we often end up making it worse."

5 • DEATH & DENIAL

"Let me illustrate what I mean," Theo continued. "Have either of you heard of Ignaz Semmelweis?"

"I haven't," Ana replied. Tom shook his head and leaned back in his chair.

"Semmelweis was an obstetrician and researcher at the Vienna General Hospital during the mid-1800s. The mortality rate was horrendous in the section of the maternity ward where he worked: one out of every ten women there died during childbirth. Their deaths haunted Semmelweis.

"The collection of symptoms associated with these cases was called *childbed fever*. It was a horrible, painful disease, and over half of the women who contracted it died in a matter of days. Can you imagine how frightening it would be to have your baby there?"

"I would've stayed home," Ana said.

"You wouldn't have been alone. In fact, this hospital had such a terrifying reputation that some women gave birth on the street and then went to the hospital.

"At the time, conventional medical science called for separate treatment for each symptom. Inflammation was thought to indicate excess blood, so they bled the patient or applied leeches. Fever was treated the same way. Respiratory problems suggested bad air, so they improved ventilation. They tried all of this to treat childbed fever, but nothing worked. The women kept dying.

"The terrible risk wasn't a secret. Patients openly begged to be moved to a different part of the maternity ward. The other section had a mortality rate of one in fifty—still awful by today's standards, but far better than Semmelweis's area.

"Semmelweis couldn't understand the discrepancy between the two sections of the maternity ward, and he became obsessed with the problem. The only obvious difference between the sections was that doctors worked in one, while patients in the other were attended by midwives. That seemed inconsequential, so Semmelweis tried to eliminate the other differences between the maternity sections.

"He standardized birthing positions, ventilation, and diets. He inspected how laundry was done. He looked at every possibility he could think of, but he found no answer. Nothing he tried made any measurable difference in the mortality rate.

"Then he visited another hospital for four months. And when he came back, he noticed that the mortality rate had improved significantly in his section of the maternity ward while he was away. It was the first real clue he had seen, and he was determined to follow it.

"But it wasn't until one of his fellow researchers developed all the same symptoms of childbed fever and died from a scalpel scratch that Semmelweis started thinking about the research done by the doctors on cadavers."

"Cadavers?" Tom asked.

"Yes. Vienna General was a teaching and research hospital. Many of the doctors split their time between treating patients and examining human remains."

"Oh no," Ana groaned.

"People didn't understand germs in those days. Doctors mostly reacted to the symptoms of their patients without fully understanding their cause. But when Semmelweis compared his own routine to that of the doctor who had been his replacement, the only difference he saw was the amount of time performing cadaver research. It was the same difference he had failed to notice between the doctor and midwife sections of the ward; midwives didn't work on cadavers, but doctors did.

"Semmelweis concluded that healthy patients were being infected with childbed fever by cadaver 'particles' on the hands of the physicians themselves. He immediately required hospital staff to thoroughly wash their hands in a chlorine solution before examining any patient. Almost immediately, the death rate plummeted to one in one hundred."

"So the doctors were the carriers," Tom said.

"They were," Theo answered. "What a crucial and painful discovery. Semmelweis wrote this: 'Only God knows the number of patients who went prematurely to their graves because of me.'

"Imagine the weight of that knowledge," Theo continued. "The physicians were doing the best they knew, but they were carrying a disease they didn't understand. All of those agonizing deaths, all of the bereaved families, all of the debilitating and horrific symptoms of childbed fever could have been prevented if the doctors had washed their hands."

Ana closed her eyes. Tom was shaking his head.

"But of the many tragedies within this story," Theo continued, "the most shocking may be this: the medical establishment at large refused to acknowledge Semmelweis's findings or adopt his recommendations."

"You can't be serious," Ana said.

Theo shrugged.

"What were they thinking? Tom exclaimed. "How could they possibly let more of those people die?"

Theo raised his glasses. "Rather than accept a painful truth that would save lives, they clung to a falsehood that kept them blameless."

Tom rubbed his forehead.

"A doctor is meant to heal," Theo said. "That's part of what makes the Semmelweis story so heartbreaking. The very people who had studied and sacrificed and worked to care for others were the ones spreading disease."

"That's awful," Ana whispered.

"It is," Theo agreed. "And this story is a stark warning. If we don't see clearly, we may harm the very people we intend to help. That holds true well beyond medicine. It applies to all human interaction. And, most importantly," Theo said, sitting down and looking from Ana to Tom, "it applies to the way you are leading."

6 • THE WAY WE SEE

"The Semmelweis story shows the danger of misperceiving the problems we encounter," Theo said. "It depicts the very human and very destructive tendency to resist admitting we are part of the problem, even when seeing and acknowledging that could lead to a solution. And I also think it's a helpful metaphor for understanding self-deception."

"Oh boy, a metaphor," Tom said, half joking. "I'm a pretty literal person."

"I get that," Theo said. "Well, let's unpack this. When I say self-deception is a disease, a sickness that targets our perception, what I mean is that it infects us with an inward mindset, a self-focused and distorted way of seeing ourselves and others. Instead of seeing other people as people like we are, with hopes and needs and objectives, we instead see them as obstacles or opportunities, or we don't really see them at all. The people and situations we encounter matter only to the degree that they impact us."

Theo peered over his glasses at Tom and Ana. "I bet you've been on the receiving end of that before. Feeling like someone only wanted something from you or saw you as a burden? Or maybe didn't see you at all?"

Tom nodded, thinking of how his daughter acted sweet and affectionate anytime she wanted something from him and how quickly she could turn sour if he refused. He mostly just gave in these days, especially since the divorce.

"Yes," Ana said, "I had a coworker once who was quick to discount the ideas I had. It felt like they needed to be right and they thought that I was just slowing them down."

"How did that impact you?" Theo asked.

"I was less willing to share my thoughts because it seemed pointless," Ana said. "And I tried to work around the person as much as I could."

"Self-deception has a disastrous impact on relationships because no one likes to be seen or treated as less than fully human," Theo said. "It's even more damaging because when we're self-deceived, we can't *see* that we're self-deceived, and we resist the idea that we are the ones with a problem, just like the doctors who rejected Semmelweis's findings. And that is exactly what was going on for me in San Francisco.

"I was so inwardly focused, so fixated on my own burdens and perceived mistreatment, that I couldn't remember how excited and lucky I had felt to be part of the project in the first place. The other people I worked with, even those I considered my friends, were reduced to being minor characters in the all-important drama of my life. And while I had plenty of excuses to explain my slipups, I didn't have an ounce of curiosity about the objectives, needs, and struggles of others. It was all about me."

"Well, you can't be responsible for everything, right?" Tom said, feeling uneasy at some of the implications in what Theo was saying. "Sometimes you just need to get your job done."

"That's the thing, though," Theo said. "Despite all the effort I was putting in, and all the discomfort I was grinding through, I wasn't doing my job, not in the way that really matters. My job wasn't just to check off the tasks assigned to me; it was to help move the project forward. Really doing my job would have meant that I was fulfilling my obligations in a way that enabled everyone else on the team to succeed—to have what we call an *outward mindset*. When I'm outward, I'm interested in the needs and challenges of the people around me, and I work hard to have the right impact on them. That is the result I am responsible for.

"The truth is," Theo continued, "that each of us is interconnected to other people, so there's no way our performance can be accurately measured without accounting for the impact we have on others. To be a parent, or a coworker, or a leader is to be in relationship with real people—people we significantly impact. And that means *how* we accomplish our work can matter as much as *what* we accomplish.

"But that's exactly what I fail to see when I'm self-deceived and have an inward mindset. In fact, it's the very thing I don't want to see. When I'm inward, I only see the negative ways that others impact me and I refuse to accept my own contributions. And, like I mentioned earlier, I even start to see others as objects to some degree, viewing them as vehicles to get what I want, or as obstacles in my way, or even as irrelevant, like they're just the background scenery in my life."

"So let me make sure I'm understanding," Ana said. "You're saying that self-deception is a problem in the way we see other people. And that, when we have this problem, we can't see that our perception of others is distorted?"

Theo nodded. "Don't see, and even refuse to see. And just like the doctors at Vienna General couldn't see how a single illness caused all the symptoms of childbed fever, people overlook how self-deception causes various types of dysfunction in organizations. It is the invisible problem that underlies all other issues."

"Issues like…," prompted Tom.

Theo rattled off a list: "Lack of accountability, procrastination, power struggles, disengagement, poor communication, entrenched conflict, entitlement, turnover, and low morale, to name just a few."

"You really believe all that is caused by self-deception?" Tom asked.

"Every people-related problem we face is created, sustained, or exacerbated by self-deception," Theo replied.

"That's a big claim," Ana noted.

"It is," Theo acknowledged. "And it's the reason we're spending this time together. If we fail to see how so many different problems in our human interactions are actually rooted in self-deception, then we waste all sorts of time and energy trying to alleviate symptoms instead of addressing the root cause. At best, these efforts help only temporarily, like relying on coffee to stay awake. And at worst—"

"It's like doctors opening a couple windows instead of washing their hands," Ana finished.

"Exactly," Theo said.

"The analogy is good and all," Tom said, "but I don't think handwashing is going to fix procrastination or employee turnover."

"Of course not," Theo said. "None of the thorny and recurring challenges in relationships and organizations are going to disappear with one simple shift in behavior. Lasting positive change requires work on a deeper level, that's why we're focusing on recognizing self-deception and moving from an inward to an outward mindset. Ultimately the way you see other people matters as much as what you say or do."

Tom was feeling skeptical. "If you can't see you have a problem, how do you even know you have it? Where does it come from?"

"Those," said Theo, "are excellent questions."

7 • THE ROOT CAUSE

At that moment, there was a knock at the door. "Come in!" Theo called.

The door swung open, and in walked Zagrum's CEO, Kate Stenarude. She looked to be in her fifties, and the room felt bigger when she entered. She gave Theo a friendly double pat on the shoulder, then shook Ana's and Tom's hands.

"I should apologize for barging in uninvited. My eleven o'clock fell through, and I thought I'd make sure Theo wasn't feeding you any falsehoods. How's it going? Where are you at?"

"Theo was just describing self-deception as a disease of perception," Ana said, "and Tom had asked what causes it."

"Oh, good," Kate said. "You're going to tell the story about your son crying? I love this part."

"Kate loves all the stories where I make mistakes and have to learn things," Theo said to Tom and Ana.

"That is 100 percent true," Kate laughed.

"Believe me, it's not something I'm proud of," Theo said, "but it does illustrate what we're about to dive into. The story Kate's talking about happened when my son David was still a baby, maybe four or five months old. It can't have been long after I came home from San Francisco.

"One night, I woke up to the sound of him crying in the room next to ours and glanced at the clock. It was 1:00 a.m. I was groggy, but I knew I should get up to comfort him and let Tracie keep sleeping.

"But you know what? I didn't get up. I knew what I should do, but I just stayed in bed, listening to David wail.

"And then, I started to think about Tracie in bed next to me, and I got mad. She knew I had an important meeting in the morning and that I needed a good night's sleep, and she was still on maternity leave, so she could catch up on sleep when David was napping during the day, right?"

Tom raised his eyebrows, and Ana grimaced.

"And was Tracie even sleeping anyway," Theo continued, "or just pretending to be?"

"Wow," Ana said. "Why not just get up? Isn't this all sort of dramatic when the only thing that needed to be done was to go take care of the baby?"

"It is a bit dramatic!" Theo said, laughing. "But I hope you recognize the sort of mental progression of sensing something you ought to do and finding reasons not to."

"Theo's story illustrates something called *self-betrayal*," Kate said. "If we think of self-deception as a disease, then self-betrayal is the germ that causes it. It is the root cause of our distorted perceptions. And unfortunately, it's extraordinarily common. We betray ourselves anytime we fail to act on or honor the helpful senses we have toward other people."

"It's the kind of thing that happens every day," Theo said. "You feel like you should offer someone an apology, but you don't. The performance of someone on your team starts to decline, and you have a sense that you should ask them what's going on, but you put it off. People start talking about someone behind their back, and you know you shouldn't join in, but you do anyway. You have a sense to wait until after a meeting to pull someone aside for a sensitive conversation, but you bring up the issue in front of everyone."

"Just the other day," Kate added, "I was at Rockefeller Center in New York for a meeting. And as I got into an elevator, I saw someone skid around the corner and dash toward us.

"I knew I should hold the doors for them, but no one else in the elevator moved, so I just let the doors slide shut and avoided eye contact. I don't know if the person was late to a big meeting or had an interview, but a few seconds of my time and they might have made it."

"Good example," Theo said. "Kate didn't hold the elevator. I didn't move to help my son. These are examples of self-betrayal."

Kate stood up and wrote a definition on the whiteboard:

SELF-BETRAYAL

Choosing not to honor our own sense regarding how we should respond to the humanity of others

"So what happened with the baby?" Ana asked. "Did Tracie get up?"

"I'm glad you asked," Theo said. "On this particular occasion, I eventually rolled out of bed and went to David's room, grumbling to myself and not bothering to step quietly. The little guy had lost his pacifier, and one of his arms had slipped out of his swaddle. It probably took thirty seconds to get him settled, and he was back to sleep.

"But it took me a long time to drift off again, thinking about the inconvenience and feeling resentful. The next morning, I was out the door before Tracie woke up. And anytime I felt tired during the day, I felt angry again.

"So even though I ended up doing the thing I had felt I should do, the way I did it and the way I felt toward Tracie were dead give-aways that I had betrayed myself."

"Well," Ana said, looking at the board, "isn't self-betrayal a strong label?"

"Yeah," Tom said. "After all, you ended up getting out of bed, and it's not like Kate sliced the tires on someone's car or did something malicious."

"A germ doesn't seem like much either," Kate responded, "until it compromises the immune system. Some examples of self-betrayal may look small at first glance, but they open the doorway to self-deception and all its accompanying problems."

8 · A TWISTED NEED

"Sometimes it's easiest to see how self-betrayal leads to self-deception by drawing it out," Theo said. He turned to Kate. "I believe a diagram is in order, don't you?" She gave a jaunty salute with the marker.

"I'll use my story for now," Theo said, "but be thinking about how the principles apply to your own circumstances, especially in or between your teams. Self-betrayal and self-deception show up here at Zagrum, just like everywhere else."

Tom and Ana nodded.

"So that night, I had a sense: get up and take care of our son before Tracie wakes up. The moment I felt that feeling, I had a straightforward choice. I could honor my sense or betray it."

Kate wrote on the board:

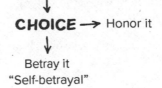

SENSE
Get up and tend to David so Tracie can sleep
↓
CHOICE → Honor it
↓
Betray it
"Self-betrayal"

"You already know how things unfolded. I hesitated to do what I originally felt to do, and that choice had an impact. How did it influence the way I saw Tracie?"

"You said you had a big meeting, right?" Ana said. "So maybe you saw her as insensitive or unsupportive."

Theo nodded. "What else?"

"Not appreciative of the work you were doing," Tom said.

Kate added "ungrateful" to the list.

"You even thought she might be pretending to be asleep!" Kate noted.

"That's right," said Theo. "Throw 'faker' up there for good measure. And if she can hear the baby but isn't getting up, what does that make her?"

"Lazy," Tom said.

"Right," Theo said. "Okay, so how do you imagine I was seeing myself in all this?"

"Hmm," Tom said, leaning back. "Taken advantage of, for sure. And hardworking."

"Maybe a bit of a martyr?" Ana offered hesitantly.

"No question," said Theo. "I thought I was getting a bad deal. I saw myself as being the bigger person, maybe even the better parent! And I definitely felt some self-righteousness, thinking about all the important things I was doing for our family."

The list Kate had written looked like this:

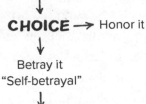

SENSE
Get up and tend to David so Tracie can sleep
↓
CHOICE → Honor it
↓
Betray it
"Self-betrayal"
↓

HOW I STARTED TO SEE **MYSELF**	HOW I STARTED TO SEE **TRACIE**
· Mistreated	· Insensitive
· Hardworking	· Unsupportive
· Bigger person	· Ungrateful
· Better parent	· Faker
· Important	· Lazy

"Kate," Theo asked, looking at the diagram, "does this sound like my wife to you?"

"Not in the slightest," Kate said. "Tracie's one of the greatest people I know."

"This distorted way of seeing myself and others, this is self-deception," Theo said. "I turned inward and lost touch with reality. My wife, who is my best friend and a remarkable woman, became a warped caricature of exaggerated flaws. And I became the tragically noble martyr, burdened by a few minutes of childcare—for my own child!"

"But you *did* get up," Tom repeated, exasperated. "Doesn't that count for something?"

"Of course," Theo said. "The baby had to be tended to. But ultimately, how we see others matters as much as what we do. Even though I eventually got up, my self-betrayal opened the door for all the negative and distorted thoughts and feelings of self-deception as much as if I hadn't got out of bed at all."

"And Theo is not alone here," Kate added. "These kinds of distortions, like inflating the shortcomings of others and magnifying our own virtues, follow self-betrayal almost every time."

"I think I've seen this playing out," Ana said slowly. "But why all the mental gymnastics?"

"You know," Kate said, "I was reading the other day that biologists assume a creature's behavior or anatomy evolved for some useful purpose, even if it doesn't seem to make any sense now. I think that applies here. How might Theo's warped perception be useful to him?"

Ana looked at the diagram, and Tom shrugged.

"I'll offer another hint," Theo said. "All my negative energy and blame and self-pity came *after* I betrayed my sense to take care of my son."

Ana's eyes widened. "Your perceptions make it seem okay that you stayed in bed."

"That's exactly right," Theo said. "My distorted views made it seem like Tracie was the one at fault. And, in a twisted way, I wasn't just looking for reasons it was okay if I didn't get up; I was even looking for reasons that I *shouldn't* get up.

"But notice this: When I first woke up and heard David crying, life was straightforward. I needed to help my son and get back to sleep. But the moment I betrayed that sense, I created a new need, one that was almost all-consuming. I needed to be justified.

"And just like that"—Theo snapped his fingers—"I am deceived. Self-deceived. I began to see myself and Tracie in ways that gave me the excuse I needed, ways that justified my self-betrayal.

"I even believed that this false, distorted way I saw myself and Tracie was the truth. I thought I was the better partner and parent in the very moment I was grudgingly looking after my son and resenting my wife. I was swallowing the very lie that I had created!"

Underneath the definition of self-betrayal, Kate wrote, "When we betray ourselves, we seek justification and turn inward."

"Self-betrayal isn't just making a mistake," Kate said. "It's ignoring an internal call to respond to the humanity of others, then hunkering down in staunch denial of our choice. It sets us on a futile quest for justification. We trade reality for a self-serving fantasy that only diminishes our capacity to connect with others and solve problems."

9 • OBJECTIONS

"Okay," Ana said, "I think I'm following. But I've been wanting to ask you both something."

"Go for it," Theo said.

"You've been telling us that when we fail to respond to our helpful senses toward others, we get into a distorted place, right?"

"That's right."

"But what about times when we're not wrong about others?"

Tom sat up taller and scooted forward in his seat.

"Tell me more, Ana," Theo said.

"Well, what if Tracie had been pretending to be asleep? I mean, what if she was mad and wanted to punish you or something? Or what if your coworkers in San Francisco had been deliberately excluding you from the updates or food plans?"

"Ah," Theo said, nodding. "I think you're asking how we can know whether or not we're seeing clearly. Are others intentionally mistreating us, or are we just perceiving mistreatment?"

"Yeah, exactly," Ana said. "I can see how it's important to question your perceptions, but how do you not drive yourself crazy by second-guessing what you see? What if the other person is actually a jerk or even manipulative?"

"They could be," Theo admitted. "It's certainly not impossible for our negative perceptions of others to align with who they are—at least, how they are behaving at that moment in relation to us."

"Seeing other people as people doesn't mean wearing rose-colored glasses and assuming everyone has innocent intentions," Kate added. "And it's not about taking responsibility for other people's choices. Abusive situations are real, and people can be legitimate victims of circumstances beyond their control, including the actions of other people."

Ana nodded.

"When we're determining how much we trust someone or whether it is healthy for us to spend time with them, the kind of person they choose to be matters," Theo said. "You don't want to hire or get married to someone who is unkind or manipulative. Remember, the truth is that other people matter like we matter, not that they matter *more* than we matter or that we matter less and should accept mistreatment."

"That makes sense," Ana said.

"The thing is," Theo continued, "in the majority of interactions we have, we're dealing with other human beings who are as imperfect as we are. But self-deception makes us more likely to see malevolent intent or animosity even when that isn't the case. In fact, we're likely to assume the worst if that gives us justification."

"And if we're trying to address our own self-deception," Kate said, "the other person's intentions or feelings toward us are actually irrelevant."

"Irrelevant?" Tom asked.

"I mean that we have a sense to be helpful to others that exists independently of anyone else's choices," Kate said. "It's our own choice to betray that sense that leads us to seek justification and become self-deceived."

"Imagine if I had immediately responded to my sense to get out of bed and care for David that night," Theo said, "without waiting or making excuses. I would have been back in a few minutes. And you know what? I bet I would've fallen asleep quickly.

"What kept me awake was my resentment toward Tracie and the self-justifying story I was telling—the story I needed because I knew I should've gotten up right away.

"So even if it somehow wasn't 'fair' for me to get up, even if Tracie *was* awake and ignoring David's crying or trying to punish me somehow, none of that would change the fact that I had felt a pull to help my son and let Tracie rest. We can't escape responsibility for the way we see others and the way we honor or ignore our senses toward them."

Tom looked skeptical.

"Let's hear it, Tom," Theo said. "What's bothering you?"

"I'm just thinking," he said, arms across his chest.

"Well," Ana jumped in, "what if you hadn't had the feeling to get up when you heard your son crying? Then it technically wouldn't have been self-betrayal, right?"

"You're not pulling any punches this afternoon, are you, Ana?" Theo smiled. "What do you think?"

"Well, it can't seem like it would've been right to roll over and go back to sleep when your baby is crying," Ana noted, "so maybe it's not the best example."

"I've got one," Tom said. "My old supervisor, Pierre, was the kind of guy who was sure he knew best. And he'd take all the credit without getting his own hands dirty, you know what I mean?

"Well one day, he came in and interrupted a meeting I was leading. He looked at some of our plans for the next product launch and loudly made some big changes. I thought his ideas were going to cause problems down the road, but I figured, 'He's the boss,' right? 'If he didn't trust me and my team, that's on him.'

"Sure enough, things went south, and because he had been so public about his plan, everyone knew who to blame. He had his tail between his legs for months, and it almost cost him his job."

As he finished his story and saw the looks on the others' faces, the satisfied smile on Tom's face drooped.

"So if I'm understanding you, Tom," Kate said, "you're saying that you didn't have any helpful senses toward Pierre. Is that right?"

"I don't remember any sort of sense to help him, no. My whole team thought he had it coming."

"Does this scenario fit the question you were asking, Ana?" Theo asked.

"Yeah, I think so."

"Can we diagram it out, Tom?"

"Sure."

"Because we're not seeing a sense here, I'll leave that part blank," Theo said. "Next, how were you seeing Pierre?"

"Arrogant, entitled, aggravating, unqualified." Tom said each word in rapid succession. "But I'm telling you, everyone else was seeing it too."

"I don't doubt it," Theo replied. "And how were you seeing yourself?"

These answers came slower. "Unrecognized...taken advantage of...overlooked...justified—shoot."

Theo cocked his ear. "What was that last one?"

Ana covered her smile with her hand.

"Justified. Fine, I felt justified," Tom said. "But I'm still pretty sure I didn't betray any sense to help or anything."

"And what do you make of that?" Kate asked.

"What do you mean?"

"Why do you think you didn't feel a sense to help Pierre and prevent things from 'going south'?"

"I told you, he was arrogant." Tom was agitated. "And he was constantly undermining how I was leading. He didn't deserve my help."

"Sounds like you found Pierre really difficult to work with," Kate noted.

"Everyone did."

"We've been looking at specific episodes that illustrate self-betrayal and how we turn inward," Theo said. "And it's helpful to slow things down and get more granular. But life isn't really a series of separate snapshots, is it? It's more like a constant stream. I suspect you had many interactions with Pierre before this incident, right, Tom?"

"More than I would've liked, yeah."

"So this episode didn't happen in a vacuum. You had a shared history that influenced how it went."

Tom nodded.

"I want to clarify an important point about self-betrayal. We notice our feelings or senses toward others only when we're open to their humanity to some degree.

"And sometimes, we're just not. We may be busy or tired or wrapped up in our own problems. But there's another reason too. We may not experience helpful senses toward others because we are already inward toward them.

"Self-deception can be like a bout of food poisoning, where the symptoms can be traced back to a single self-betrayal. That's a problem, to be sure, but it's also fairly straightforward to understand and correct.

"The far more dangerous variant of self-deception isn't episodic," Theo said. "It's chronic."

PART II

LIES THAT BLIND US

10 • CHRONIC STRAINS

"When we're free from self-deception, we see others clearly," Theo said. "We understand and are responsive to the fact that they have needs and aspirations and fears and relationships that are as real and tangible as our own. We have an outward mindset.

"But when we are self-deceived, our view of others is distorted. As we discussed before, when we are inward toward others, they become objects to us, typically in three kinds of ways: as vehicles we can use to get what we want, as obstacles that are in our way, or as irrelevant to us.

"This objectifying view of others is evident in drastic and horrible situations, like abuse or neglect. But it also appears more subtly. We treat a cashier at the grocery store like some sort of food-scanning robot, or we try to butter someone up with insincere flattery. While each of these instances may look very different, they all share the same dehumanizing root of objectification.

"We know we shouldn't see and treat others this way. But we do it all the time. So you can see why we seek justification within the alternate reality of our self-deception, right?"

"I dunno, Theo," Tom said. "Isn't it a bit strong to call it objectification if you're just trying to get through the grocery line?"

"Have you had a customer service role before, Tom?" Kate asked.

"No, not really. My dad owned a small store I worked at before college, but I mostly stayed in the back."

Ana chimed in, "I worked tables at a diner when I was in high school. Best and worst job I ever had."

"Why's that?" Kate asked.

"I really enjoyed the people watching, and it was fun getting to know some of the regulars. But…"

Ana's face flushed, and she fidgeted with the edge of the table.

"Well, it wasn't the greatest atmosphere. Some customers made offensive and inappropriate comments. I told my manager and shift lead at first, but they'd say things like 'Don't be so sensitive. This is how the world works. Just appreciate the tips.'"

"I'm sorry that happened to you, Ana," Theo said.

"Yeah, me too," she replied. "And I wish that job was the only place I'd seen it."

Tom cleared his throat. "My daughter just applied for some part-time jobs as a food server. I'd hate if that happened to her."

"No one should experience harassment or discrimination at work, or anywhere else for that matter," Kate said. "And objectification is intrinsic to those kinds of mistreatment."

"In response to your earlier question, Tom," Theo continued, "I'd say no. I don't think objectification is too strong a label to use when we see people only in terms of how they impact us. Anytime we choose to reduce another human to a two-dimensional character in our own story, it's an act of objectification."

"Of course, there are differences in degree and severity," Kate clarified, "but it's important to see the connection. Otherwise, it's too easy to think the problem is only in other people or in extreme cases."

Tom nodded.

"Like I mentioned," Theo said, "we can have a sort of bout of self-deception, where a specific self-betrayal leads us to a distorted view of another person in a certain situation. But self-deception can also be a sort of chronic condition, and that happens as we adopt and carry with us false views of ourselves in relation to others."

Kate nodded. "Our chronic self-deception takes one of two forms: we see ourselves as either better than others or worse than others. And while that may sound simple enough, seeing ourselves as better or worse than others distances us from the truth that others matter like we do. Both can be used to provide us with justification."

"For example," Theo said, "when I was inward toward Tracie, I found justification by viewing myself as better than her. I had important things to do the next day. And my job was important for our family. My sleep was clearly a higher priority than Tracie's. At least, that's what I was telling myself.

"I felt resentful about her slow response to our crying child, even though I was still in bed myself. And I had even uglier emotions too. I felt like I was entitled to totally uninterrupted sleep, like it was something Tracie *owed* me but didn't deserve herself. And all these emotions signaled that I was seeing myself as better than Tracie."

Tom was examining his thumbnail.

"But I could have also easily found justification by flipping the script and seeing myself as worse than Tracie," Theo continued. "Any ideas what that could have looked like?" He moved to the whiteboard, drawing a new box with a line down the center.

"Well," Ana said slowly. "Maybe you think you're not great with the baby or you don't know what you're doing. You could worry you'll just make things worse."

"And if Tracie has to get up anyway, why bother?" Tom said. His voice held an edge that wasn't lost on Theo, Kate, and Ana. "Everything she does is perfect," Tom continued, "and she'll probably let you know it."

"Exactly," Theo said, finishing this new diagram.

MYSELF	TRACIE
• Not great with the baby	• She gets up anyway
• Don't know what I'm doing	• Everything she does is perfect
• Just make things worse	• She'll let me know I didn't do it right

Ana looked troubled.

"On the surface, these two situations seem like night and day. But feeling better than others and feeling worse than others actually perpetuates the same dynamic. Both are ways of being inward and staying focused on ourselves. Both are lies we use to seek justification when we betray ourselves. And both warped views can follow us into different situations and be a type of chronic self-deception."

"You've said that a few times," Ana said. "I want to make sure I'm following. What exactly do you mean by 'chronic self-deception'?"

"I mean that we carry around the false views of ourselves that we use to justify our self-betrayals. Then we no longer need a specific instance of self-betrayal to spark justification and self-deception. We experience all the negative symptoms of being inward because we are *already* inward. We carry the lie that we are better or worse than others with us into new circumstances as a false self-image that will keep us from seeing the people around us."

"And that means we stop experiencing helpful senses toward them," Kate said. "We can't see their humanity because of the lies we bring into our interactions. Why would you stoop down to help someone you think is beneath you? Or, on the other hand, if you're convinced other people are better than you, why would they need anything you could offer?"

"Ugh," Tom said. "So this all means that I didn't feel an impulse to help Pierre because I was already inward toward him?"

"I'll let you speak for your own experiences," Theo said, "but I wouldn't be too surprised if self-deception was at play in your story. It sounded like you were happy about Pierre failing, even though it came at the expense of your own project."

Tom opened his mouth, then sighed. "I guess it doesn't make much sense looking back on it. Sitting back to watch Pierre flop made quite a mess of things."

"Each of us can have a tendency toward seeing ourselves as better or worse than others depending on the relationship or circumstance," Kate said. "But both positions are falsehoods. We may very well be better or worse than someone else in a given skill or capacity, but that doesn't translate into being a more or less worthy human being. And we're much more accurate at assessing abilities when our vision isn't obscured by self-deception."

"You know," Theo said, standing and picking up a marker, "one of the easiest ways to spot these chronic self-deceptions is to pay attention to the emotions that usually accompany them."

Theo drew two squares on the board and labeled one "Better Than" and the other "Worse Than." "For example, if I see myself as better than others, I may feel entitled, mistreated, unappreciated, or resentful." As he spoke, Theo added these to the "Better Than" box. "You can imagine the impatience and frustration I might experience. But what emotions might I feel if I carry a worse-than self-image?"

"Discouraged?" Ana said. "And maybe even jealous of people you see as superior."

"Without question," Theo said. "And for me, feeling powerless and resigned is a pretty telltale sign that I am seeing myself as worse than," Theo said, completing the second box.

BETTER THAN	WORSE THAN
If I see myself as better than others I may feel:	**If I see myself as worse than others I may feel:**
Entitled	Discouraged
Mistreated	Jealous
Unappreciated	Powerless
Resentful	Resigned

"When I was in high school," Tom said slowly, "my buddy's mom died. And I didn't have a clue how to talk to him about it, and I felt awkward, so I just didn't say anything. I told myself I didn't want to make it worse or something like that. But I still regret not reaching out when it mattered. I think that I was self-focused in a worse-than way."

"Thanks for that example," Theo said. "It's not always easy to see or admit to our justifications.

"Now, there's more to explore with all of this," Theo said, "but I think it's about time to break for lunch. Thank you for being here, Kate."

"Thanks for letting me join in," Kate said. "And," she continued, turning to Ana and Tom, "it is so good to have both of you on the team. We are grateful you're here."

"Well," Theo said, pushing his chair back from the table, "Tom and Ana, I'll see you back here in an hour."

As everyone stood, Kate turned to Tom. "Do you have a minute to chat?" she asked.

11 • SABOTAGE

"Sure," Tom said, his mind scanning the morning's events for reasons why the CEO would pull him aside. He hated being caught off guard.

"Great," Kate said. "Can we walk to my next meeting while we talk?"

"No problem."

"How are you settling in?" Kate asked, interrupting his thoughts as they moved toward the elevator door.

"Oh, fine," Tom said. "It's been a whirlwind for sure, but I'm excited to be here, and I've got a great team."

"And outside of work?"

"No complaints," Tom said. "Though I do wish someone had given me an instruction manual for parenting a teenage girl."

"Ah," Kate said. "I mostly watched that from the sidelines as my nieces were growing up. Some parts didn't look easy, but they all turned out great. And, believe me, if my brothers can do it, you can."

"I sure hope so," Tom said.

"What do you think about what you've been exploring with Theo today?"

"It's been interesting. But I'm surprised that you and Theo would spend so much time with us, especially with all you've got on your plate and all the growth you're managing." Kate smiled.

"I know it's not typical, but we've learned that when you hire great people, and they internalize the ideas you're exploring, our jobs become much simpler."

"Makes sense," Tom said as they walked out of the building toward an adjoining one.

"Tom, I want you to know that we're excited to have you here. We feel strongly that you're the right person to help our product team stay at the cutting edge of the industry."

"Thank you. I'm grateful for the opportunity."

Kate nodded. "I also want you to know that what you're learning with Theo and Ana is as important to your success here as all your other skills and experience. It's not enough to be brilliant or knowledgeable, not without also having a positive impact on the other people around you."

"Right, of course," Tom said, a knot growing in his stomach.

"When I heard about your experience with Pierre, I was concerned about your past getting in the way of your ability to lead here."

"About that," Tom interjected, "I get that it wasn't my finest moment."

"And we all have those experiences. In fact, your story about Pierre reminded me of my experience early on here at Zagrum. I was part of the senior leadership team, and I reported to Lou Herbert, our founder. By the way," Kate said, interrupting herself, "have you met him yet?"

"Not yet. But I've heard the stories."

"Good! Well, I hope you get to meet him soon. Lou's one of the best leaders I know. But he wasn't back then. And he'd be the first to admit it." Kate sat on a bench and motioned for Tom to follow suit.

"In fact," Kate continued, "it got so bad, I decided to quit. And not just me. Five of us on the executive team left at the same time. But Lou begged me to reconsider, and coming back was one of the best decisions I've ever made."

"Why did you choose to come back?" Tom asked.

"Well, for a while, I thought it was because Lou changed. I wasn't sure it would last, but he really transformed for the better."

And that's the difference, Tom thought. *Pierre Cardon is never going to change.*

"But that wasn't the whole truth," Kate said, pulling Tom out of his thoughts. "I had been disgusted with Lou. I thought he was rude and abrasive and acted like he was smarter than the rest of us. I knew he was the problem.

"But what I didn't realize, not until a long while after Lou showed up on my doorstep and apologized, was that I was self-deceived too. Don't get me wrong, the way Lou viewed and inter-acted with us was a problem. He really could be demeaning. But I had to realize that someone else's poor behavior doesn't justify my own.

"My inwardness might have looked different on the surface, but underneath it all, Lou and I were the same. I could see all the ways he was destroying the company, and I was convinced I was bet-ter than him. I totally overlooked the ways I had recruited people against him—and not just other executives but my whole team. Lou might have been sabotaging the company, but so was I. His better-than inwardness showed up as blustering arrogance, but my better-than inwardness showed up as self-righteousness and was damaging the company just as much, maybe more. I was simply a little more likable in the way I went about destroying this place.

"I came back because I wanted to help save the company. After some reflection, I knew we both needed to change, but I also knew that all I could control was me. What Lou would do was for Lou to decide."

Kate stopped talking, and Tom didn't speak for a while.

Eventually he sighed. "I don't talk about this much, but I was laid off from my last position. I had been there for almost ten years and I thought my contributions were obvious. But apparently they weren't. It's eaten at me every day since."

"That you were let go?"

"That they laid me off and kept Pierre. But I was doing the same sort of recruiting you were talking about, Kate. People love to hate on an arrogant supervisor."

"I know," Kate said, smiling. "And that's the sort of thing we can't let happen here."

"I hear you," Tom said.

Kate was smiling. "So now what?"

"What do you mean?"

"What are you going to do about that situation with Pierre?"

Do? Tom thought. *What am I supposed to do?*

"Well, we don't work together anymore," he stammered. *Could you say anything more obvious, Callum?* Tom berated himself. "And we didn't have much of a relationship anyway..."

"Spend some time thinking about it," Kate said, "and see if there's anything you feel you ought to do. Part of being a fully responsible leader in the present is taking responsibility for the times you've fallen short in the past."

Tom was stunned. No one had ever spoken to him like this before. He felt both called out and hopeful.

"Thanks for your time, Tom," Kate said, standing and extending her hand. "Your success matters to me. Please don't hesitate to let me know if I can help in any way."

12 · PIVOT

Theo's phone buzzed. "Kate!" he said, picking up the call. "Did you leave something behind?"

"I just wanted to tell you about my conversation with Tom. I felt like I could help him, given my history."

"I'm glad you pulled him aside. How'd it go?"

"Good. I asked him to try and think more about his old manager. It seems like the things you've been talking about are sinking in, and I'm thinking he might need some time to put it into practice."

"Do you think I should pivot to open up some time this afternoon?"

"Feel it out, and see what you think. I trust your judgment. But if Ana is ready, too, it might be useful to give them an invitation and opportunity to apply things."

"I agree," Theo said. "That tends to be the most helpful next step. And with Ana, my gut tells me that feeling better than others is not her challenge, at least at work."

"I think you're right. It seems like it's the opposite struggle for her. I'm running to a meeting but can talk later if you want to brainstorm further. Good luck, Theo!"

13 • SELF-IMAGE

"Welcome back," Theo said after Ana and Tom were settled. "How was lunch?"

"It really is mind-blowing how many emails can pile up in four hours," Ana said, sounding almost out of breath.

"Hopefully you're all caught up," Theo said, laughing. "Ready to dive back in?"

Theo moved to the whiteboard and uncapped a marker.

"I'd like to summarize what we've talked about thus far. What stands out from this morning?"

"That we are either seeing others as people or as objects," Ana said as Theo wrote.

"Objects in what way?" Theo asked.

"As vehicles that we use, or as problems, or not mattering at all," Tom said.

"Right," Theo said as he wrote "vehicles," "obstacles," and "irrelevancies" on the board.

"And why are we sometimes so invested in seeing others as objects?" Theo asked.

"Because we betray our own sense of what we should do for them," Ana said.

"Yes," Theo said. "And what do we need when we betray ourselves that we didn't need before?"

"Need?" Tom asked.

"Yes, what becomes most important to us after self-betrayal? What do we need?"

"Oh, right," Tom said. "Justification. Surprised I forgot that one."

"That need for justification can feel consuming," Theo said, "and we find it by seeing ourselves and others in distorted, untruthful ways. In particular, by seeing ourselves as better than or worse than others."

"And that's the chronic self-deception you were talking about," Ana said. "Self-betrayal is a moment in time, a specific choice to turn inward that we try to justify, but if we're walking around believing that we're better or worse than other people, we're already inward toward them so we won't have senses to help because we don't really see them. Is that right?" Ana trailed off, unsure. "Actually, could you talk a little more about how that works, Theo?"

"Happy to. You know, it's not like we walk around consciously telling ourselves that we are better than or worse than others. I mean, it could be overt like that, but it typically tends to be more subtle.

"When I'm seeing myself as better than or worse than others," Theo continued, "it usually shows up around specific traits or qualities that I use to find justification. Remember the distorted ways I saw myself as better than in that episode with David and Tracie?" Theo said, pointing to the first self-betrayal diagram from that morning. "Hardworking, important, the bigger person? A good dad?"

Tom and Ana both nodded.

"*These* are the sort of images of myself that I not only believe when I'm self-deceived but that I become invested in having others believe about me too. So, I'll start to portray myself in these ways because they offer me justification. I need other people to validate these false self-images, and I'll react poorly if they don't.

"In San Francisco, part of the reason I couldn't see how I was hurting the project was because I needed to protect my image of myself as hardworking and dedicated. And I would guess that part of the reason the Vienna doctors refused to accept Semmelweis's findings was because those findings threatened the image they had of themselves as competent healers."

"Well, none of those things are bad, right?" Ana said. "I mean, it's good to be competent and dedicated and hardworking."

"Of course. But there's a big difference between wanting to *be* a certain way and wanting to be *seen* a certain way," Theo replied. "When appearance becomes more important to us than reality, other people are relevant to us only insofar as they reinforce or threaten the images we are trying to portray. And in each of these examples, it was precisely this preoccupation with portraying positive traits that got in the way of realizing those traits.

"The physicians rejected discoveries that would have protected their patients and made them more competent healers because they didn't want to admit ignorance or a mistake. And trying to project my image as a 'dedicated martyr' in San Francisco was preventing the kind of collaboration and commitment that the firm actually needed. Does that make sense?" Theo asked.

"I think so," Tom said. "Like if I care so much about looking smart, I won't ask questions even though it would make me more educated."

"That's exactly right," Theo responded.

"But all the examples you gave were of positive traits," Ana noted. "What happens if someone believes something negative about themselves?"

"Important question," Theo said. "We talked about how I could've found justification by seeing myself as worse than Tracie." He pointed to the other diagram. "She had more experience with children than I did. When I held David, he often ended up crying even harder until he was with his mom. I sometimes felt ashamed and incompetent as a dad. I could have let all that justify my hesitation, allowing my belief that I wasn't good enough to stop me from even trying to help my son. So if those were parts of my self-image, and I saw myself as incompetent or inexperienced, how do you think it might impact me in other situations?"

"You might not be confident enough to try things," Tom said, "or you might be quick to give up."

Ana was quiet for a while, then added, "You wouldn't want people to see you that way. You'd probably try to hide it. You'd be worried that the ways you're seeing yourself are true and afraid that other people would find out. Like you're a fraud."

"Right," Theo said. "And I'd spend precious time and energy trying to make sure no one finds out that I'm not as capable as I try to appear. My life may even feel like a kind of performance."

Ana didn't say anything.

"When I have distorted views of myself," Theo continued, "they will infect every interaction. They may be better-than selfimages I want to validate or defend or worse-than self-images that

I want to hide away for fear of getting found out. But either way, I'm not seeing myself clearly in relationship to others. I'm focused more on appearance than reality. I'm inward. And that sort of chronic self-deception is at the heart of most relationship challenges, not to mention most leadership failures."

The air in the room felt heavy.

"That's a lot to think about," Theo said, breaking the silence. "I think we'll wrap up for the day. I'd like to give you time to put into practice the ideas we've been talking about. I'm guessing you've been thinking about someone you've been at odds with, a relationship where there's friction?"

Ana and Tom both nodded.

"Think, for a moment, about any ways you haven't been seeing this person clearly. Are you feeling better than or worse than them? Are you thinking of them as an obstacle in your way or a means to an end?

"Try to see the person you're thinking about as a person who is as real as you, who has needs and hopes and real challenges. While you're doing this, pay attention to any sense you have about what you should do. And then," Theo said with a wide smile, "go and do what you sense you should do."

"Today?" Tom asked.

"Of course," Theo said, smiling. "Today."

14 • FIRST STEPS

Tom looked down at his phone, then sighed. He had been putting this off most of the afternoon, but Kate and Theo were right. He did feel like he owed Pierre an apology. Not that Pierre didn't have anything to apologize for himself, but that was the same sort of loop he'd been stuck in.

Maybe I don't even have his number anymore, Tom thought, but sure enough, it was still there in his contacts.

The phone rang. Once. Twice. Three times. *Leave a message? Or call again?* Maybe he'd just send an email. That'd be fine. Then the call connected.

"Hello." Pierre's voice was flat.

"Hi, Pierre. It's Tom Callum."

"Tom Callum." There was a pause. Then, in the same flat tone, "What can I do for you?"

"Look, I don't want to take up your time, but I've been thinking about things today, and I owe you an apology."

Tom didn't wait for a response, speaking into the silence. "I wasn't as supportive as I should have been, especially on the Wilkens' project last fall. I made some assumptions about the information you had, and I let my ego keep me from putting our project first. I'm sorry for that. And I'm sorry I wasn't easier to work with."

"Okay," Pierre said after another pause. "Well, thanks for your call."

"Yeah, sure. Take care," Tom replied. He hung up the phone and groaned. It didn't look like they were going to grab drinks anytime soon, but at least he could say he tried. And he felt better, actually. He gathered his things and headed home.

Ana was tired after navigating rush-hour traffic. She walked in the house and felt her fatigue deepen. The living room was a mess, toys and books and other signs of short attention spans scattered around. The house was quiet, though, almost suspiciously so. Then she heard joyful shrieking from the backyard.

Through the kitchen window, she saw her kids, Mateo and Miranda, running around the yard as her husband, Jaime, sprayed them with the hose. They were all soaked and laughing. She hated missing moments like this.

And she also hated being the one who couldn't stop her brain from seeing all the inconvenience the summer fun created. It meant the kids hadn't eaten yet, and it likely pushed them to a later bedtime, which meant less time for her and Jaime, and—she jumped as a spray of water hit the window in front of her face. Jaime grinned at her, and the kids giggled and waved. She blew a kiss and went to grab some towels.

The evening went as Ana expected, late bedtime included, and she could barely keep her eyes open by the time she and Jaime had a moment of quiet.

"How was your day, mi amor?" he asked. "That big training going okay?"

"It's interesting. I'm with that coworker I told you about, the one who thinks he has the only good ideas. Oh," she said, suddenly remembering, "did you have that interview today?"

"No," Jaime said, "I didn't think it was a good fit. I told you I'm happy with the freelance work for now. It gives me time with the kids."

But not enough time to help them clean the living room or to make sure dinner is ready on time. She felt guilty at the thought, especially remembering how happy the kids looked. But still, she pursed her lips, letting the silence speak for her.

He knew she thought he could do more.

Jaime started to speak, then sighed and let it drop. That had been happening more often lately, like they didn't have the energy to put the argument into words. Despite how tired she was, it took Ana a long time to fall asleep.

15 • TRIAL & ERROR

Tom cursed under his breath the next morning when he saw the incoming call from his ex-wife.

"Where are you, Tom?" Laura's voice was cold. "Becca's going to be late for school. You were the one who insisted that weekend custody starts Friday morning, remember?"

"There's not any chance you could..."

"I have a career, too, Tom. I'm already at work. But I can ask Brian if you..."

"No, no. I'm on my way. Bye." Tom turned his car around and raced toward the house he used to live in. He called Theo.

"Theo," Tom said, "I'm going to be about half an hour late this morning. My daughter missed the school bus, so I need to drop her off." It wasn't entirely untrue. Becca could've taken the bus, and it sounded better than "I forgot it was my day to pick up my only child."

"Thanks for letting me know," Theo replied. "Drive safe, and we'll see you when you get here."

Becca was radiating annoyance when he pulled up.

"You know the bus gets kids to school, too, right?" Tom said.

"The bus smells bad, and you have to leave like forty minutes early," she responded.

"I'm going to be late to an important meeting," Tom fumed.

"Just leave me home then," Becca snapped.

"I'm not going to do that. Put on your seat belt. I just want you to know that your choices affect other people too."

Becca rolled her eyes.

"Man, I hate when you do that," Tom said. He turned onto a main road and started to accelerate.

They drove for a few minutes in silence. Becca pulled out her cell phone, and Tom heard Theo's voice in his mind: *"Are you seeing any of the people around you as objects?"*

He sighed. "Look. I'm sorry for getting mad. There's this work training, and the CEO is probably going to be there, so I guess I'm on edge today."

Becca didn't look away from her phone.

"Would you put the phone away, please?"

She shoved the phone into the top of her backpack and looked out the window. It was a new backpack and an expensive phone. He wanted her to have nice things.

"Anything going on at school today?" Tom forced his tone to stay light.

Becca shrugged. "Nope."

"What about afterward? Play practice?"

"It's called rehearsal. And I don't know if I still wanna go."

"What? I thought you liked it."

Becca shrugged again.

Like pulling teeth, Tom thought. He took a breath and tried one more time.

"Do you already have plans tonight? We could go see a movie or something?"

"Stop being weird, Dad. Ever since the divorce, I've been, like, your project or something. I'm fine, okay?"

Tom didn't say anything. When they pulled up to the school, Becca sprang out of the car, slammed the door, and didn't look back. *Maybe the whole "see people as people" thing only works on fully developed adults*, Tom thought.

16 • LIMITATIONS

A few minutes after Theo got off the phone with Tom, Ana entered the room.

"Good morning!" Theo called cheerfully. "Tom is running about a half an hour late, but we can get started. How are you doing? How was your evening?"

"It was all right, thanks. I'm glad to get the chance to talk with you," Ana said. "There's some things I've wanted to ask about."

"Sure," Theo said. "What's on your mind?"

"When I was driving home yesterday, I started thinking about how each car around me had a person inside of it, or even whole families," Ana started. "And they were all going somewhere, which means they'd been somewhere, and it could have been their grandma's house or the hospital, and they all have lives and feelings and loved ones waiting for them to arrive. And it just... I mean, it's beautiful, too, but I feel like I can't hold that all the time. It's exhausting."

She was slightly out of breath when she finished talking.

"I know exactly what you mean," Theo said.

"We keep talking about how important it is to see the humanity of others," Ana continued, "and it feels like you're asking us to care about all the people we interact with all the time. But I've already got my kids and husband, my extended family and friends and neighbors and coworkers. I'm spread thin as it is, even without trying to remember everyone's humanity during rush hour!"

"How do you feel as you're talking about this, Ana?"

"Discouraged, mostly. Tired. Maybe guilty."

Theo nodded. "It sounds like you're wondering how we can see the humanity of others without feeling burned out or overwhelmed. Is that right?"

"Exactly," Ana said. "Seriously, if you're seeing everyone around you as people, won't you get slammed with things you should do for them?"

"It's a balance, to be sure," Theo responded. "Sometimes there are competing priorities we have to sort out, and no one has endless time or energy."

"But couldn't that just be a justification?" Ana pressed.

"Yes," Theo said simply. "And the truth is, only you will know for sure. But in my experience, self-betrayal is followed by rapid-fire justifications and feelings such as annoyance or frustration. Other times, I've had a sense that I wasn't able to act on, but I felt at peace about it.

"I remember once seeing someone barely miss the train I was on. I couldn't do anything about it except to sympathize for the frustration they must have felt and hope they got where they needed to go. Sometimes honoring our senses toward others is as simple as seeing them and extending well-wishes.

"I want to make sure we stay realistic about all this," Theo continued. "We all have limitations. It's a part of being human, and that can include feeling guilty, overwhelmed, inadequate, or discouraged at times. I've been there too. But those feelings don't help us be more responsive to the humanity of others. They can easily turn us inward."

"I see that," Ana said. "But then it can be hard not to just feel bad for feeling inadequate or overwhelmed."

"Which would only be deepening a self-focused spiral," Theo said. "What I'm trying to clarify is that when we say that *others* matter like we do, it also means that *we* matter like they do. Staying open to the humanity of people around us doesn't mean carrying the weight of the world or ignoring our own needs. It doesn't mean that we shouldn't prioritize and sometimes say no to what others ask of us. It doesn't even mean never feeling frustrated or overwhelmed. It's about not getting bogged down in those self-centered feelings and looking beyond them to see and connect with others. Does that make sense?"

Ana nodded.

"We may not be able to do everything, for everyone, all the time," Theo continued. "But we can focus on seeing and responding to the people right in front of us."

"Yeah, the people right in front of us," Ana repeated. "Well, that's another challenge I've been struggling with. I think I need some advice."

17 • PORTRAYING & PRETENDING

"Happy to help if I can," Theo replied. "What's on your mind?"

"You asked us to think about someone we're having a hard time with—a relationship where there's friction. And I, well, I kept thinking about Tom. He's been hard for me to work with."

"Tell me more," Theo said.

"I don't want to be negative or gossip, it's just..." Ana sighed. "He talks about that boss he couldn't stand, and it's like he's describing himself. He has an immediate opinion and zero reservations about sharing it. It's abrasive, especially when his opinions are unsolicited and outside his area of expertise. I'm trying to understand and apply what we're learning, but I have a hard time not seeing Tom as a problem."

"Thanks for trusting me to help you explore that," Theo said. "To start, let me ask you this: Would you say that you tend to see yourself as better than or worse than others?"

"Hmm. That feels hard to answer so directly since I know neither is a good response." Ana shook her head. "But I think I mostly feel worse than others at work. I worry about not knowing enough or not making the right calls. I can get stuck on my mistakes. But the funny thing is I feel all the better-than emotions at home, like impatience and resentment, especially when I don't think my husband pulls his weight."

She thought again about the night before and how annoyed she had been with Jaime. She loved that he was laid-back and family focused. Well, she loved it most of the time. She'd known she needed a partner who was quick to laugh. But sometimes, she wished they both ran at the same speed.

"That's not uncommon," Theo said with a smile, interrupting her thoughts. "We all find justification in different ways with different people in different environments. But you're saying that, in general you feel less than others at work. Is that true toward Tom?"

"I'm not sure," she responded.

"Well, let me ask this," Theo continued. "Are there any qualities that you admire in Tom?"

"I think he knows his stuff," Ana said. "And I think he knows where he's going. People like to follow that. It seems like his confidence can give other people confidence too."

"So he's knowledgeable, confident, has a clear sense of direction," Theo summarized.

"Yeah, I think that's true."

"Interesting that some of those strengths might be tied up in the very traits you find difficult in Tom," Theo said. "Our strengths and weaknesses usually aren't opposites. The line between confidently knowledgeable and abrasively opinionated can be thin."

Ana nodded. "You know, as we're talking about this, I think the thing that might bother me most is that some part of me believes that the way Tom acts is what leadership should look like. Assertive, certain, straightforward. I often find myself hesitating or second-guessing my choices, which doesn't seem like the greatest trait in a leader."

"Where do you think the hesitation and second-guessing comes from?" Theo asked.

"I…" Ana paused. "Some of it is probably just my personality. Ever since I was a kid, I've wanted people to like me and wanted to belong. But when you're always trying to avoid upsetting other people, you can get out of touch with your own opinions.

"I also haven't seen many leaders who look like me. I feel a lot of pressure to try to blend in, but at the same time, you have to stand out and prove that you belong, especially in sales. Sometimes it's like I'm acting out a part or wearing a mask. Like you said yesterday, life can feel like a performance—at least at work."

"I think I understand some of what that's like," Theo said. "I was the only African American student in my graduating class at law school. I tried to make sure other people wouldn't stereotype me, so I was always early to class and careful about how I dressed. If everyone else went casual, I was business casual. I didn't want anyone to see me unprepared or even struggling. I carried a lot of worry about being negatively categorized in ways that would harm my career chances. It's not an easy additional weight to carry."

"No, it isn't," Ana said. "I worry about being perceived as arrogant or aggressive, so sometimes I don't speak up confidently, even when I do know something, to avoid negative labels. I think that might be some of what makes it hard for me to work with Tom. I resent how easy it seems to be for him to speak his mind."

"I'm curious, Ana," Theo said. "What do you think it's like for the people on your team when you're worried about being seen as arrogant or aggressive?"

"Well, I don't think they're getting the real me. It's a cautious or filtered version."

"And consequently," Theo said, "you might not be getting the real them."

Ana nodded.

"What else?" Theo asked.

"I'm sure it's not as energizing as it could be. You know what it's like to work on a project with someone who isn't thinking about themselves? They're just free, focused on the project, and connected to other people. That's exciting and fun. And it lifts you up just being around people like that."

"I know what you mean. That's what it's like for me to work with Kate."

"She seems like that sort of person," Ana said. "I wish it felt more like that with Tom."

"What do you think it would take? To feel that sort of energy and freedom in your work with Tom?" Theo asked.

Ana laughed. "The first things that come to mind are ways I wish he were different or would change. But I don't think those are the sort of answers you're looking for."

"I do find that focusing on the things we can actually control tends to be more empowering and effective," Theo responded with a smile. "Which isn't to say that Tom isn't responsible for how he behaves. He has areas where he can improve too. But given the qualities you said you admire in him, what if you were to give advice to someone just like you who was working with someone just like Tom?"

Ana thought for a minute. "I'd say learn all you can from them. And don't feel threatened or intimidated."

"That's great advice," Theo said. "It can be hard to shake the self-focused worry of an inward mindset, particularly if someone else's strengths seem to shine a spotlight on areas where we aren't confident. The more we get worried about being seen in a certain way or become focused on our weaknesses, the less able we are to focus on the project and people we work with. Reframing our situation as an opportunity to learn is a much better response. Though," he chuckled, "it's easier said than done."

Ana smiled, then looked thoughtful. "I know I am a much better leader when I'm not focused on looking like a good leader. And I can see that some of my struggles with Tom could be from comparing areas he's good at to ones I'm working on. But I'm not sure how to feel more confident or free as a leader. I can feel stuck between that fear of being perceived as abrasive and fear of not being decisive or confident enough. How do I get over that?"

"What you're talking about is more common than you'd think," Theo said. "It's actually pretty easy to talk about changing behaviors—do this, don't do that. But when you talk about changing mindset, it's trickier, even counterintuitive, because it's not just a matter of effort. If the problem is an inward mindset, the solution can't be more focus on ourselves, even if we're trying to cure ourselves. You don't get to an outward mindset by gritting your teeth and trying to force yourself to think about others, because that can still just be about you."

"Okay," Ana said slowly.

"The people you were describing who help others feel energized and excited, they're less worried about or focused on themselves because they are so curious about others and so engaged in the projects they are working on with others. Becoming free of chronic self-deception—better than *or* worse than—doesn't happen when we focus on ourselves. We become self-deceived when we lose sight of the humanity of others. We are only freed by seeing and focusing on the humanity of others.

"I want you to experiment with it today and just try to see Tom as a person. Not putting him on some sort of pedestal or ignoring things that bother you, but paying attention and seeing if you can find any moments of genuine curiosity. It's a gift to offer others, and it would be nice if they would offer that first, but just try and see what happens."

"I will," Ana said. "Thanks, Theo."

"And remember," Theo said, "we didn't hire you to be Tom, Ana. We need the skills, experience, and strengths you bring. We hired Tom, and we also hired *you*."

18 • OLD PATTERNS & PROGRESS

"Tom! Welcome back!" Theo boomed. "How'd the drop off go?"

"Fine," Tom said tersely. "Sorry I'm late."

"Not to worry. Ana and I made good use of the time," Theo replied. "I wanted to ask how your homework went. Anything to share?"

"Well, yesterday afternoon, I kept thinking about that story I shared about my old boss, Pierre. At first, it was on my mind because I regretted bringing it up. It's not my finest career moment. But then I was thinking about how I let a personal grudge hurt a project that my team had put time and effort into. They deserved better, no matter how arrogant or difficult I thought Pierre was.

"And, after talking to Kate yesterday, I realized that I owed Pierre an apology. Kate challenged me to call him up, so I did."

"What did you say?" Ana asked

"I felt clumsy and was pretty direct about it." Tom laughed. "I don't think he knew what to think. The conversation didn't last very long at all, and I thought it was a bit of a dud, actually. But this morning, I had an email from him thanking me for the call and wishing me success."

"How do you feel about it?" Theo asked.

"Better," Tom said. "Lighter, even. I didn't realize I'd been carrying it around. But then this morning, I picked up my daughter, and…anyway."

Tom stopped, hesitant to go into what had happened that morning with Becca.

"You're among friends," Theo encouraged.

"Well, it was a pretty rocky car ride," Tom began and told the others what happened.

After Tom finished, Theo asked, "Where do you think the conflict or negative experience with Becca started, Tom?"

"It felt like she was ready for a fight before the car started moving. And even though I tried to connect and not see her as a challenge, it really didn't pan out."

"Where do you think you contributed to how things went? Was there any way you were seeing her that might've had an influence?"

Tom felt himself start to get defensive, then he paused. *I don't think Theo is attacking or judging me right now.* "I was definitely feeling inconvenienced, and I didn't even try to hide it. I'm sure Becca didn't want to be late either, but my own day and plans felt more pressing to me than hers."

"That's good awareness," Theo said. "It's not easy to try something new. And we often build patterns of interaction that resist change, especially in our closest relationships."

"You know, actually," Tom said, "even though it's true that she could've taken the bus, I had said I'd pick her up today and forgot. I think I should've just owned that from the beginning, and it would've probably made things go better. I was pretty defensive from the get-go. I've clearly got work to do."

"Join the club!" Ana said, surprised by Tom's honesty.

19 • EXCUSES & BLAME

"So," Theo said, "let's review our premise thus far. One of the most pressing problems that a leader, organization, or individual faces is self-deception. It is a condition where your perception is systematically distorted in your favor. We also call it having an inward mindset. Most of us won't even see that we have this problem because we need the twisted perception to feel justified when we fail to see and respond to the humanity of others. To find justification, we tend to view ourselves as either better than or worse than the people around us. All clear on that?"

Ana nodded, and Tom reached for a snack.

"To prop up our distorted view," Theo continued, "we use logic to accuse others and make excuses. The more plausible our blame and excuses are, the better they fuel self-deception. 'I shouldn't be expected to reach out and introduce myself. I'm the new hire around here!' or 'I can see that there's an issue here, but addressing it isn't in my job description.' Or even 'I'm not going to intervene; they need to learn the consequences of their actions.'

"We blame others by focusing on their faults or exaggerating our own virtues. But it's all fodder for justification, a means to excuse our own self-betrayals.

"Now, our excuses can be pretty sophisticated. We'll claim that certain values like efficiency, or fairness, or common sense constrained our choice. We try to make our self-betrayal look rational, understandable, or even virtuous, as though placating a jury of our peers."

"So how do you tell whether you're justifying a self-betrayal or just considering extenuating circumstances?" Tom asked.

"Great question. In fact, Ana and I talked about that this morning. I think one indicator is how willing I am to take responsibility for my own contributions and choices. When we're pursuing justification, we tend to either deny all responsibility or make a strategic, partial concession with a large caveat attached. 'I may have messed up, *but*…justify, justify, justify.'

"Another difference between justification and context is what we pay attention to: Are we trying to deepen our understanding of where others might be coming from? Or are we grasping for anything to prove they deserve to be blamed?

"But mostly, Tom, it just feels different. I know what it feels like to be defensive, and I know what it's like to simply explain what happened. I know the difference between acknowledging what led to a mistake and dodging responsibility."

Tom nodded. "Yeah, those do feel like different things for sure."

"Some of the most common indicators of self-deception are blame and excuses," Theo said. "They rapidly infect a culture, turning our focus away from results. All the time, energy, and creativity that could—and should—be going toward problem-solving, collaboration, and innovation gets funneled toward justification instead. It leads to the kind of downward spiral that crippled Zagrum in the company's early days.

"The good news is that accountability can spread in a culture, too, especially when it's modeled by a good leader. Can I tell you about one of my role models?"

"Of course!" Ana said.

"Her name is Gia Chen. She's a federal judge now, but I met her when she was a fourth-year attorney and my project supervisor. One of our firm's biggest clients was looking to acquire land for a high-density housing project. The location they wanted was occupied by trailer parks, so my job was to become an expert in California mobile home law to make sure we weren't blindsided by anything. It seemed pretty straightforward: the project had local support, even among some tenants of the park, because the area wasn't well managed at the time.

"It was an important and fraught time in Gia's career. By your fourth year, you're supposed to be seasoned, trustworthy, and competent. Any mistakes at that point could ruin your chances of making partner in the firm. So the pressure was on.

"I started researching, and it was all good news. I wrote a hefty memo about why it wouldn't be an issue to acquire the land. Gia was happy. Our client was happy. I felt good.

"But two weeks later, Gia and I were going over some detail or another when she said, 'Oh, I've been meaning to ask: Did you check all the pocket parts during your research?' And my gut sank."

"Pocket parts?" Tom questioned.

"Yes," Theo said. "Legal books can be hefty and expensive to print, so back in the day, to reduce the costs of frequent updates, most books included a pocket in the back where relevant legal changes were stored.

"When Gia asked about it, I felt sick. I hadn't checked the most up-to-date information.

"We ran to the firm's library and, sure enough, the laws had changed in a major way. I had given our client a green light for a path leading right toward a legal, financial, and bureaucratic nightmare.

"We went back to Gia's office, and she called the lead partner on the project. 'Jerry, you remember that expansion analysis? Well, I made a mistake. It turns out that the law has recently changed, and I missed it. Our expansion strategy is wrong.'

"I was dumbfounded. It wasn't Gia's mistake. It was mine. But she—with a lot on the line—was taking responsibility for the error. Not once on that call did she blame me.

"After she hung up, I said, 'Gia, I was the one who didn't check the pocket parts.'

"She smiled at me. 'That's true. You should've checked them. But I'm your supervisor. Several times during the process, I had thought to remind you but didn't get around to it. If I had done that, we wouldn't be here. You made a mistake, but so did I.'"

"Wow." Tom whistled. "That's impressive."

"Right?" Theo said. "She had obvious reasons to blame me, and she would've been totally justified.

"But what's truly remarkable is the fact that she didn't *need* to be justified. She wasn't afraid of being defined by a mistake or fixated on protecting her own image.

"She kept sight of the fact that she and I both were fallible humans. She focused all her energy on correcting course and minimizing damage. And, by acknowledging her own minor contribution, I felt about a thousand times more willing to take responsibility for my much larger mistake." Theo shook his head. "I would've walked through a brick wall for Gia.

"Later that afternoon, I wrote Jerry a long email about how the whole thing had been my mistake and how incredible Gia was as a supervisor." Theo smiled. "Jerry read some of that email to the firm a few years later at the party we threw when Gia made partner. She had earned the firm's unanimous support."

"She sounds like a great boss," Ana said.

"She was," Theo said. "And that's the kind of leader we need you to be too. We want to be a blame-free organization, but that requires a remarkable level of accountability. And it starts with leaders."

"No pressure, right?" Tom said to Ana.

"Nothing you can't handle," Theo said. "Let's break for an early lunch today. When you come back, we'll dive into how self-deception spreads and what to do about it."

"Sorry again for delaying things this morning," Tom said.

"Believe me," Theo said. "What you are doing to try to put all this into practice outside of this room will be far more important than anything that happens in this room."

PART III

THE VISION TO LEAD

20 • TWO WAYS

When Ana and Tom returned to the training room, Theo was laughing with a white-haired man. The newcomer must have been in his late seventies, but he still had the ramrod-straight bearing of a marine.

"Ana, Tom, welcome back!" Theo called. "We won the lottery today. This is Lou Herbert, our former CEO. He'll be joining us for the afternoon."

"Hello, Ana. Hello, Tom," Lou said. "Theo has just been telling me how much he's enjoyed spending time with you both. It's a pleasure to meet you."

You couldn't hide from Lou's eyes, Tom thought. But somehow, you also didn't need to. It was like a searchlight that left you warm instead of exposed.

"What are you doing here?" Ana asked. Then her face flushed. "I didn't mean that the way it sounded."

Lou had a well-worn smile that his entire face took part in. "I come in every so often to see how things are going. Keeps me out of trouble."

"Lou is being characteristically modest," Theo said. "He's on our board, and his experience is invaluable. Many of our biggest customers have stayed with us for decades because of him."

"You are pretty famous around here, Lou. And at my old job too," Tom noted.

"Well, if I've earned any sort of recognition," Lou responded dryly, "it's probably a 'most improved' award; I've had plenty to learn and relearn.

"I have to admit, though, I envy you two having access to Theo and having time set aside to explore all of this. Poor Kate had to help me bumble through things as we went."

"You two blazed a good trail!" Theo said. "I could tell this company was different after my second time meeting you, Lou. Remember?"

"You'll have to remind me, I'm afraid."

Theo turned to Ana and Tom. "I came to Zagrum sixteen years ago. I had left the law firm to become general counsel and then COO of a company that Zagrum acquired. Not too different from your story, Ana. And because I knew a lot about the intellectual property acquisitions, I joined the executive team."

Lou nodded. "That's right."

"In our first meeting, I was given several difficult assignments to complete before the next meeting, two weeks later. It was a heavy load at any time, but especially given the circumstances. My family had relocated for the job, and there were plenty of stressors with that transition. The night before our meeting, I had one task left, but I was exhausted, and it seemed minor, so I let it go.

"As I reported on my progress the next day, I focused on all I'd done and the unexpected challenges that had arisen and casually mentioned the task I hadn't gotten to. This ringing any bells, Lou?"

"Not remotely, no."

"Well, Lou was leading the meeting, and without any fanfare, he asked Kate to take the assignment I had left undone. The meeting continued with other reports, and I noticed that no one else had left a task unfinished.

"I felt embarrassed and small and couldn't wait to get out of the room to lick my wounds. But Lou caught me before I could slip out and asked if he could walk me to my office. He was about the last person I wanted to see right then."

Lou chuckled.

"But I wasn't going to turn down my new boss, the man who had taken a mediocre company and made it into an industry powerhouse. And along the way, Lou got me talking about the move and how my family was adjusting."

"Ah," Lou said. "Tracie had a hard time being farther away from her parents, I believe."

"That's right," Theo said to Tom and Ana. "Lou even called our home and spoke to Tracie later that night just to see if there was any way he could help. It meant a lot to her.

"When we got to my office, Lou put a hand on my shoulder and looked right in my eyes. 'Theo,' he said, 'I want to talk to you about that assignment. I know you are working hard, and you're doing good work. I hope you know that.'

"'But, when you take on an assignment, not following through has a ripple effect. People are depending on you delivering what you committed to do. If you know that you aren't going to be able to keep a commitment, reach out, ask for help, let people know. We need you to be thinking about your impact on others.'"

"How'd you take it?" Ana wondered.

"Somehow I wasn't offended or defensive. I was inspired. I found myself thanking him for talking to me."

"I've never been known to beat around the bush," Lou confessed.

"So what's the secret, Theo?" Ana asked. "Why did that approach work? Is it because he led with some compliments?"

Theo smiled. "I've thought about that. It wasn't because of anything he said, Ana. There wasn't a strategy. It's not a formula. It worked because I could feel that Lou was really honest with me *because* he saw me as a person and wanted me to succeed.

"How a leader sees others is more important than anything they do or say. In fact, the success or failure of any given leadership technique hinges on understanding that every behavior can be done in two ways—inwardly, with a focus on ourselves and the way others impact us, or outwardly, caring about others and our impact on them.

"People can tell if we're inward and seeing them as objects instead of people. No matter how much someone tries to fake it, you'll eventually know how they see you. If Lou had been pretending to care about me and my family, even if he had asked the exact same questions, I'm certain it would've come through."

"I had a coworker once," Tom said, "who would often give compliments, but it didn't feel genuine. It was like they had some personal agenda under the surface."

"That's the feeling," Theo said. "People can say or do all the 'right' things, but the place it comes from makes all the difference. And by the same token, someone could be unpolished and imperfect at offering feedback and still have it land well because you can tell that they care about you."

"Like your experience with Lou," Ana said.

"Yes," Theo said. "Exactly."

"Kate pulled me aside yesterday," Tom said, "and talked to me pretty directly. But I could tell that it was because she really wants me to succeed. As uncomfortable as it was, I am so grateful she did that."

"I have learned a lot from Kate," Lou said. "She really sees people."

Theo nodded. "It's a big reason she's such a successful leader. When we're outward, people know it.

"But having an outward mindset doesn't mean overlooking others' shortcomings. Lou didn't let me off the hook for dropping my assignment, but he also didn't reduce me to *being* my mistake. I was inspired to be better because Lou and I both knew I *could* be.

"It would've been easy for me to call someone else on the executive team and ask for help to get that last job done or to ask which of my tasks were most urgent if I wasn't able to do them all. Instead, I didn't ask for help or give anyone a heads-up, and then I justified my choice. The way that Lou saw me made it easy for me to own that mistake."

"And since then," Lou added, "we've done a better job at helping people know what exactly they're responsible for, who is relying on them, and how it all connects to the success of the company. Right, Theo?"

"Absolutely," Theo said. "We've become much more intentional about clarifying job expectations and showing people the interconnectedness of our operations. That has been critical in helping Zagrum thrive. People ought to know why their work matters and who it impacts."

"I'm still impressed by how you knew what to say to Theo, Lou," Ana said. "And I've heard other stories where you seemed to know if someone needed discipline or encouragement and how to offer it. How did you become the kind of leader who can sense that sort of thing?"

Lou rubbed his weathered cheek and took a deep breath. "I had to really change the way I saw others. I nearly lost everything I love."

21 • CONTAGION

"I'm pained by how much of my life I spent failing to see and respond to the humanity of the people around me," Lou began. "I was so deeply self-deceived that I felt like the whole world was against me. My employees didn't care enough, work hard enough, think smart enough. My wife didn't show enough appreciation or support. My son—" Lou paused. "My son was an embarrassment to our family, wasting his potential almost out of spite. Everything was everyone else's fault. I was convinced I deserved better.

"Eventually things came to a head, and it all happened at once. Cory, my boy, was caught using drugs his senior year of high school. I almost didn't speak to him for the entire time he was in youth detention, and things didn't get any better when he came home. He was rude and belligerent, and he broke our family rules. Within three months, he was arrested again and went to a treatment program.

"At the same time, five of my six executives walked out of the company, including Kate. I later learned that some people in the company were calling it the March Meltdown. I couldn't believe they would abandon me like that, after all I'd given them.

"I was hopelessly lost, unable to see how I was contributing to the conflicts in my deteriorating relationships.

"And the relationship where I felt most justified and blameless was with my son. I tried all the punishments and rewards I could think of with Cory, but it all backfired. It took me a long time to understand why."

Lou's mouth twisted. "No matter how often I claimed that what I was doing was for Cory's own good—the grounding, the bribes, the lectures, the curfews—the truth was that each of my responses was inward. It was all about me.

"I wanted our family to be viewed in a certain way, wanted our neighbors to think the Herberts had it all together. Cory's behavior threatened that. And it threatened my identity as a successful parent. He was ungrateful, and spoiled, and undisciplined. He was an obstacle to the life and reputation I was trying to create. The truth is, I cared about my image more than our relationship.

"It's the same mistake I was making at work," Lou continued. "I claimed my actions were all for the good of the company, but my ego was at play. Some part of me was threatened by the competency of others. I felt like I had to prove that I deserved to be CEO, had to defend my image as the 'right man for the job,' so I shot holes in other people's ideas and seized control instead of trusting them."

"I bet that went over well," Tom said.

"About as well as you'd guess," Lou said. "Anytime you objectify others, you provoke resistance. I wasn't letting my leaders lead. My own self-image was more important to me than our company's success. And my executive team was tired of feeling unseen and unappreciated, and so they left.

"Looking back, though, it's almost funny how unsurprising the escalation was, both at work and at home. I wasn't seeing my son or my team as people, and so they resisted me in just about everything I did.

"Most conflicts follow this same predictable pattern. Objectification invites objectification. Justification provokes justification. Blame and excuse spark defensiveness and counterblame. The inward mindset is as contagious as the common cold."

"What Lou is saying is critical to understand," Theo said. "When we are self-deceived and inward toward others, we invite them to be inward in return. And what else could we expect? If we don't see and care about their humanity—their needs and wants and hopes and fears—if we are indifferent, manipulative, or even hostile toward them, then their defensiveness, resistance, and hostility should come as no surprise."

"But what is truly fascinating and terrible," Lou said, "is how we use the negative responses of others—the very behavior that we helped provoke—as further evidence to support our distorted views of them.

"We call this dynamic *collusion*, where two inward parties are mutually inviting the very behavior or response they claim to resent in the other, almost as though they both had agreed to keep the cycle going. It's the way that self-deception can spread like a sickness."

Lou paused. "I'm curious," he said. "Where have you seen collusion show up here at Zagrum?"

Tom and Ana looked sideways at each other, each wondering what the other was thinking.

The room was oddly quiet.

"What is it?" Lou asked. "Believe me, nothing can shock this old cat."

"Well," Tom said slowly. Then, thinking better of it, he looked at Ana. "Should we talk it through now?"

"As good a time as any, I guess," Ana said, unconvinced.

"The collusion is between our two teams," Tom said.

"Of course!" Lou said with a smile. "The old Product and Sales collusion!"

Tom and Ana shot each other quizzical looks.

"That one comes back to life every few years if it's not carefully watched," Lou said.

"Well, it's alive and well," Ana said, only slightly relieved.

"Okay, then," Lou said. "How do you know it's a collusion?"

"Well," Ana said, "because both of our teams are contributing to the problem."

"That's a solid indicator. But collusion is even more involved than that," Lou said. "When parties in a conflict are inward toward each other, it's almost like they've decided to work together to keep the conflict going. Let me describe how it played out between me and Cory, then we can look at the dynamic between your teams."

22 • COLLUSION

Lou stood up and moved to the whiteboard.

"A few weeks after Cory returned from youth detention, he asked me to use the car. I didn't think my son deserved any privileges, and I didn't trust him at all. But I could feel my wife's pleading eyes, so I made a condition I was sure he'd refuse.

"'You can take the car, but I want you home by ten o'clock.' He was an eighteen-year-old boy, and it was a Friday or Saturday night. I was ready for his protests, but Cory surprised me by saying, 'Okay. Thanks, Dad!' The screen door slammed behind him.

"My wife wanted to watch a movie together, but my team was playing, so she read a book instead. I couldn't keep my mind on the game. I was certain Cory would ignore the curfew, and I kept watching the clock. And in my mind I was sharpening my lecture for when he came home late.

"As the evening continued, I found myself more and more frustrated. Frustrated at Cory's choices and what all of it meant for our family. Frustrated he couldn't see that I only wanted the best for him. Frustrated that he wouldn't even keep this one small commitment.

"By 9:58 my anger had burned down to a sort of weary resignation. And then, I heard tires squeal in the driveway. Cory burst in with a huge smile, threw me the keys and yelled, 'Made it, Dad!'"

Lou shook his head. "That could have been a beautiful moment—a chance to recognize and praise Cory's effort, to tell him how glad I was that he was home on time. It was an opportunity to strengthen our relationship. But instead I felt a keen pang of disappointment. And you know what I said?

"'Sure cut it close, didn't you?'"

Lou paused. "What must it have been like for my son? To come home from detention, facing the stigma and shame of public mistakes, only to be met by a father who could barely stand to look at him? It's no wonder he went searching for other places to feel accepted.

"And, as you can imagine, my response didn't encourage Cory to make curfew in the future. Why would he try if he was treated poorly no matter what? That type of interaction had become characteristic of our relationship. We were in collusion."

Lou drew a box with four quadrants on the board. He wrote "Lou" over the left side and "Cory" over the right.

"Why do you think I had a hard time seeing my son as a person? What was Cory doing that was so frustrating to me?"

"Well, doing drugs, for starters," Tom said.

"Talking back, breaking family rules, being disrespectful," Ana said.

"And getting arrested," Theo said.

"Okay," Lou said, writing these answers in the bottom right quadrant. "And how do you think I saw Cory when he did those things?"

"Well, if you were curious, you might have wondered whether he was acting out for attention or something," Ana said.

"Right!" Lou said. "I *could* have seen that. But I didn't because I didn't really *see* Cory. I was inward toward him."

"So maybe you saw him as irresponsible," Ana suggested.

"Yes. What would you say, Tom?" Lou asked, writing Ana's answer in the bottom left-hand quadrant.

"I'd see a disrespectful punk," Tom said, thinking of his own teenager.

"It's not easy to admit," Lou said, "but I saw my son as a failure." The words were stark on the board: irresponsible, disrespectful, failure.

"And how was I acting toward Cory?" Lou asked, moving to the next quadrant on the board.

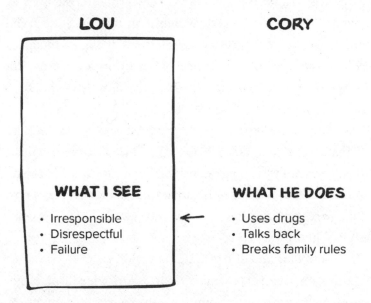

"You said you tried all the punishments and rewards you could think of," Ana said.

"Lectures, bribes, laying down the law," Tom added.

Lou finished writing "punish," "reward," "lecture," and "bribe" in the top left quadrant and turned to the group.

"Now," Lou said, "I'm not crazy about punishing, lecturing, or the rest, but I don't have much of a choice, do I? If Cory wasn't doing the things he was doing, I wouldn't have had to do the things I was doing! I was trying *everything*, but I wouldn't have had to try *anything* if I just had a son who was responsible to begin with."

"Couldn't Cory be asking the same thing, though, just reversed?" Ana asked. "Like, 'I wouldn't have to talk back if my dad would listen to me' or something like that?"

"I think you're right," Lou said, smiling. "Of course, no parent is ultimately responsible for what their child chooses. But even so, things might have gone very differently if my son had felt seen and heard by me. I couldn't see my contributions, though. I thought I was doing all these things because of what Cory was doing. But why was I really doing them? What's the link between Cory's actions and my own behaviors?"

Tom's eyes were fixed on the diagram. "The way you saw Cory."

"That's right," Lou said. "That's the key. I would have said that I was doing what I was doing because of the way my son was behaving. But the truth is, I was doing what I was doing because of how I chose to see my son. And, in return, how do you think Cory saw me, given how I was acting?"

"As controlling and distrusting," Tom said.

"And with how you changed tactics," Ana added, "he might have seen you as a dictator some days, then a pushover on others. Or at least as inconsistent."

"Anything else?' Lou asked.

"Unloving," Tom said quietly. "Impossible to please."

Lou added these to the fourth quadrant on the board, completing the diagram.

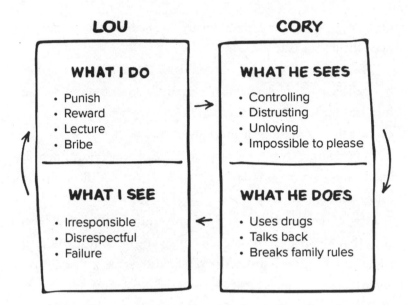

"And when Cory interprets my actions as dictatorial and unloving, his disrespectful and rebellious responses make sense, don't they?"

"Which then gives you more justification to tighten your grip," Tom said. "That's the cycle you were talking about."

"Exactly right," Lou said. "I was provoking Cory to behave in the very ways I said I hated. I was disappointed when he came home on time the night he took the car because, as strange it sounds, I actually *needed* him to be late. I wanted the justification that I could only have if he continued to be the problem I thought he was. You know, if you would have asked me just moments before he arrived home what I wanted most, I would have told you that I wanted my son to come home safe and on time. But it turns out that what I wanted most was to be justified. And him coming home on time got in the way of that. Anytime we blame someone else, we need them to be blameworthy.

"This is what happens in collusion. And Cory's frustrating behavior was understandable given the inward way I viewed him and the ways I acted toward him. We were giving each other excuses to continue a cycle that only hurt us both."

Theo added, "Cory and Lou provided each other nearly perfect justification, almost as if they collaborated to do so. That's why we call it collusion."

"Right," Lou said. "It's as if we crave justification so desperately that we say to each other, 'I'll mistreat you so that your bad behavior toward me is justified, if you'll mistreat me so that my bad behavior toward you is justified.'

"Of course, making that sort of agreement would be absurd. But when people are in collusion, they can't see the twisted way they are working together to provoke ongoing mutual mistreatment."

"It's not that we enjoy problems," Theo said, "and it's also not to say that we are responsible for the poor behavior of others. But when we're self-deceived, justification becomes our highest priority. And often, whatever we are complaining about is the very thing that justifies us, so we turn a blind eye to our own contributions and fixate soley on the mistreatment we receive from others, reinforcing a belief that in many circumstances is a lie: the belief that the other person we're in conflict with is entirely worthy of blame and we are completely in the right."

"But what was Lou supposed to do then?" Tom asked, exasperated. "Sit back and let his son do drugs? Stand by while he ruined his life?"

"Of course not," Lou said. "But my problem wasn't in trying to discipline or correct Cory. In fact, I felt an obligation to intervene and help my son. But," Lou said, holding up two fingers, "there are two ways to do almost any behavior—with an inward mindset or with an outward mindset.

"My problem was that I was inward toward Cory. I wasn't seeing his full humanity, and my self-centered motivations tainted my other actions. How likely is anyone to accept correction from someone who sees them as a failure or an embarrassment?"

"When we're inward," Theo said, "it is almost impossible to invite positive change. Each action and choice we make is undermined by the distorted and self-serving ways we're seeing ourselves and others."

"Right," Lou said. "My inwardness toward Cory was mostly manifest as forceful attempts to discipline."

"And that usually backfires," Tom said.

"Right," Theo said. "But it isn't just the behavior, it's the underlying mindset too. Lou could have adopted totally opposite tactics and still have been equally inward and equally ineffective."

"Exactly right," Lou said. "If I had been more permissive of Cory because I was afraid of confrontation or wanted to be seen as nice or cool, it would have been just as self-centered as my impatience and frustration. And when we're not seeing others as people like we are, our influence won't just be ineffective. It will be destructive.

"But I didn't understand that—not until we took Cory to a treatment program in Arizona."

23 • FEAR & FEELINGS

"I was trapped inward at home and at work," Lou continued. "When we took Cory to treatment, the parents were all required to attend a meeting. I assumed it would be to brief us on how they were going to fix our kids. Instead, it taught me some of what you have learned here.

"Although," Lou chuckled, "I fought it tooth and nail. I couldn't be the one with a problem! I owned a company. I had my act together! But eventually, with the help of some remarkable people, I started to see more clearly.

"And I didn't like what I saw: a leader who was so sure of his own brilliance that he micromanaged and suffocated the brilliance in others; a husband who took his wife entirely for granted; a father"—Lou's voice broke—"a father so unyielding and disapproving that he couldn't see how much his sensitive, creative, beautiful boy yearned for his approval."

"It was one of the most painful and hopeful experiences of my life. Because recognizing my contributions meant that I could finally change things."

"When you lay it all out like that," Tom said, gesturing to the collusion diagram, "it seems so obvious. But I'm still having a hard time understanding why things get so tangled up. I know it happens—I told Theo and Ana yesterday about an old supervisor I wanted to see fail, even though it hurt my own team's project—

but what keeps us so fixated on justification when it only makes things worse? It doesn't make sense!"

"You're right, Tom," Theo said. "It really *doesn't* make sense, not from a more clear-sighted perspective. It's like trying to make sense of a nightmare after you wake up. It's only within the distortion that the falsehoods appear convincing."

"What do you think?" Lou asked. "Why do we put so much of our energy and effort into justification, even when it drives collusion? Even when it doesn't get us anywhere helpful?"

"I think," Ana said, "that sometimes we're just afraid."

"Say more," Lou encouraged.

"I mean, it can be scary to own up to what you've done—when you knew what you should do and you didn't. Maybe we're afraid that our self-betrayal defines us—that it means we're bad or petty or selfish or incapable."

"Or maybe even afraid that other people will find out, and we'll be punished or rejected or lose their respect and admiration," Tom said.

"Great insights," Theo said. "When we betray ourselves, fear can drive us inward, motivating us to find justification within a falsehood.

"But the fear is an illusion too. It's a result of being inwardly focused. It keeps us from accepting responsibility and admitting our mistakes, even though those are the very actions that build trust and move us forward. It is a cruel irony that when we let an inward mindset and fear guide us, we end up pushing people away and creating the very realities we're most afraid of."

"I didn't want my son to get into trouble or to distance himself from us," Lou said. "But the cloud of my disapproval and distrust certainly didn't make him want to spend time at home. And I didn't want my leadership team to fight each decision or quit, but who would want to stay somewhere they were micromanaged and criticized? My inward mindset fed collusion and caused endless problems."

"When we're inward," Theo said, "we blame and accuse others with our thoughts, words, behaviors, and even our emotions. And all of it can fuel the deception."

"Will you say more about the emotions part?" Ana asked. "Words and behaviors—even thoughts—all seem like things we can choose, at least to some degree. But emotions seem like a different category to me."

"Emotion is connected to perception," Lou replied. "We are afraid when we perceive danger, angry when we perceive an injustice, resentful when we perceive mistreatment, right?"

"That makes sense," Ana said.

"But because self-deception is *itself* a problem of perception, our feelings can reflect and deepen the fantasy."

"For example, Ana," Theo said, "imagine you had some delay on the way to work this morning, but your cell phone died, and you somehow couldn't get ahold of us. After a while, Tom and I would see that you were late. Your absence would be a fact; the interpretation, of course, is not. Ideally, we'd both feel concern, assuming that you had a good reason and hoping you are okay.

"But if we're inward, the way we interpret these facts will be drastically different. For example, if I was seeing myself as worse than others, I might feel insecure, thinking you didn't show because I blew it yesterday. Tom, on the other hand, might have more of a better-than self-image and feel superior, happy to be seen as the more reliable new manager. Whatever emotions we felt, they wouldn't actually be based on the facts of the situation.

"The feelings would be reflections of the distorted views of ourselves and others that we brought to the situation. I would experience your behavior as threatening to my image as a good facilitator, and Tom would experience it as a boost to his self-image as the most committed manager. Of course, both of these are interpretations that have more to do with us than with you, and they might be completely disconnected from reality. The different emotions he and I experienced would be very real but not a reliable guide to the truth of what was really happening."

"So rather than believing that our emotions say something objectively true about reality," Lou added, "it can be much more productive to recognize that our emotions say something true about our *perception* of reality.

"This is a critical distinction because understanding this difference enables us to acknowledge a feeling without allowing our knee-jerk emotional responses to assert themselves as the whole story."

"Instead of drawing an immediate conclusion like 'I'm angry because you made me angry,'" Theo offered, "a more honest reaction might be 'I'm angry because I think you meant to embarrass me' or 'I'm angry because I think you're blocking what I want.'"

"In that first interpretation," Lou noted, "there's nothing to be done. The other person has all the power. But in the other ones, I have space to question and explore. Did the person actually intend to embarrass me? Or was I reacting defensively about some aspect of my self-image that was threatened? Why do I think they were trying to make my life harder? And, maybe most importantly, do I want to be angry? Why am I choosing this?

"When we fail to take responsibility for our emotions, it's often because we don't question or take responsibility for our perception. Does that help, Ana?"

She nodded, jotting down some notes.

"When we pay attention to our emotions this way—as indicators of our perception instead of proof that someone else is blameworthy—they can help us realize we're being inward. Impatience, entitlement, disdain, and similar emotions can suggest that we're seeing ourselves as better than others, while envy, anxiety, or resignation can indicate that we're seeing ourselves as worse than others."

"I knew emotions couldn't be trusted," Tom said.

"That's not exactly what we…" But then, Theo saw Tom's smirk and chuckled.

"Oh man," Ana sighed. "I've been in a collusion without even realizing it."

"Tell us more," Theo invited.

"There's someone on my team I've been unimpressed with since I got here," Ana said. "I felt like she was lazy and disengaged. And she'd come up in multiple conversations with other team members, so I knew that I wasn't the only one who saw her as a problem.

"But I didn't want to bring anything up with her directly. There's been plenty going on with the merger, and I just didn't want to deal with it. But I'd been getting more and more annoyed with her.

"Last week, we had a meeting with the entire sales team, and I asked her to present on the project she had been working on.

This is ugly to admit, but I think I wanted her shortcomings to be shown publicly so I wouldn't feel bad about letting her go.

"But she did a phenomenal job presenting, and the presentation itself was excellent. I mean, first class. I should've felt relieved or excited to see her shine because her role is important. But instead, I felt…," Ana paused, "embarrassed? Even suspicious. Like I wondered if someone else prepared the presentation for her."

"So why are you seeing it as a collusion, Ana?" Theo asked.

"Well, I thought she was disengaged, and part of me knew that I needed to have a conversation about expectations and get on the same page. But I didn't. And I'm seeing now that by avoiding that conversation, I was provoking her to disengage more. I even stopped inviting her to some meetings that she should've been in, given her role. I was mad at her for being disengaged while at the same time preventing her from participating. Seems pretty obvious that I've been driving the dynamic I was complaining about. I didn't want to be mean or confrontational, which is why I didn't talk to her. Now I see that I was just protecting an image I cared about rather than caring about her."

"What would you say that image is?" Theo asked.

"I think I wanted to be seen as a likable manager," Ana answered.

"That's an excellent discovery," Theo said.

"And brave to own up to it," Lou added. "On the surface, not wanting to be mean or confrontational seems like a positive motivation. But leaders have an obligation to help others improve. Shirking it is neither helpful or kind."

"Right," Ana said. "But hard to see any of that when you're in the middle of it."

"What do think you should do about it?" Lou asked.

"I've got to own it. I can see that."

"If this employee is here," Lou said, "would you go take care of that today?"

"Today?" Ana asked, clearly caught off guard.

"No time like the present!" Lou said, smiling.

24 • SEEING CLEARLY

After a short break, the four of them were settling back in when Tom turned to Lou. "So how did you turn things around? Kate obviously came back, and the company has thrived. I'd guess things got better with your son too. What did you do to fix things?"

"There's a lot that doesn't work to cure self-deception," Lou noted. "In fact, most of our attempts to fix our problems don't work. We can try to change others or grudgingly cope with them, we can communicate more or distance ourselves, we can practice new techniques and behaviors, and after all this, absolutely nothing changes for the better. The painful reality is that the majority of leadership interventions fail."

"Good pep talk, Lou." Theo grinned.

Lou smiled. "Well, let's be honest. The reason most attempts fail is because they're focused on the wrong thing: they're focused on changing behaviors, not addressing mindsets. They're focused on the symptoms, not on the problem itself."

"Which makes sense," Theo added, "because unproductive behavior is so often what signals that a problem exists in the first place. It's tempting to think, 'If we can just get them to meet deadlines or speak up or change whatever they are doing that's causing an issue, then the problem will be solved.'"

"But the change doesn't stick, or the problem shows up in a different way," Lou added, "because the underlying issue wasn't addressed."

"Like with Semmelweis," Ana said.

"Exactly right. The problem of self-deception is deeper than behavior," Lou continued. "So the solution has to be too. If we want to cure inwardness, objectification, and blame, break free from collusion and escape the lies and self-images that exacerbate dysfunction, we need to first see clearly.

"Once I woke up and started really seeing the people around me, I knew exactly what to do," Lou said. "And more importantly, I was able to do it in an outward way that actually made a difference because it wasn't contrived or self-centered."

"They say a proper diagnosis is half the cure," Theo said. "But when it comes to collusion and self-deception, it's almost as if the diagnosis *is* the cure. When we see others clearly, the most helpful steps to take become clear. In some cases, being outward will mean that we take a more gentle approach with others than we have in the past. But in other situations, being outward will mean just the opposite. Where we have indulged poor behaviors in others, seeing them as people will help us be more direct and straightforward. Often hard behaviors are more helpful—like setting boundaries and enforcing consequences. But, again, the 'right' behavior only works when it comes from the right mindset."

"I had a long list of apologies to make," Lou continued, "to Cory, to Kate, and to others. I asked for feedback regarding what it was like to work with me, and I listened longer and deeper than I had before. I adjusted my efforts to try and have a better impact. Those steps alone made a remarkable difference."

"Lou's experience is a great example," Theo said. "It demonstrates how the cure to self-deception is simple to say and hard to live: turn outward. That means getting curious about the people around you and honoring the outward, helpful senses you have toward them. It means letting go of any belief that you are better than or worse than others. Because then, you don't have to waste time feeling inadequate or blaming other people. You don't misplace precious energy trying to present a facade that you are nice or successful or competent. When you're outward, you can simply be invested in the work you're doing with people who matter like you matter."

"It's that easy, huh?" Tom said.

Lou smiled. "It's a helluva lot easier than the way I used to live. I was an expert at mining for justification, but it never satisfied. My life has been more rich and fulfilling—and my work immensely more productive—the more I see and respond to others."

"Just to be clear," Theo chimed in, "turning outward isn't a one-time achievement. It's a practice. Over and over again, Lou and Kate and I have to catch ourselves in self-deception and justification and come back to clarity. All of us have to notice and set aside the chronic self-images we carry around so that we can really be *with* people."

"And there's no better time to practice than the present!" It was clear to Tom and Ana that this "no time like the present" mantra was one of Lou's favorites. "Are you two ready to tackle that collusion between your teams?"

"Let's do it," Tom said.

"Ana?" Lou said. "What do you say?"

Ana exhaled. "I'm sure we could use all the help we can get."

Theo stood up, drew a new four-quadrant box, and wrote "Sales" on the left and "Product" on the right.

"All right, this could be a little risky," Theo said. "There will be opportunities to take offense and turn inward. Are you two sure you're ready?"

Tom and Ana looked at each other.

"We're good," Ana said. Tom nodded.

"All right," Lou said. "Let's start with you, Tom. What is your team doing that is so frustrating to Sales?"

"Well," Tom said, "it sounds like we aren't as open to feedback as Sales would like, especially to what they're learning from customers."

"What else?"

"That we're not straightforward. What did you say yesterday?" Tom asked, turning to Ana. "We just send back jargon to avoid giving real answers?"

"Yeah, it just feels like excuses that are intended to be confusing," Ana said.

"Got it." Tom paused. "I think that's about it. Oh, and that we're slow to respond to product requests."

"Okay, great," Lou said as Theo added the last statement to the bottom right-hand quadrant.

Theo smiled. "And given all that, Ana, how is your team seeing Product? What did you say yesterday?"

"Arrogant, out of touch with the customer, and hard to work with."

Theo wrote this in the bottom quadrant on the Sales side of the diagram.

"And seeing Product this way, Ana," Theo asked, "what does your team do?"

"Well, we tend to push harder by sending more emails and submitting formal requests. Either that or we shut down. Depends on the team member, I guess.

"And I'm embarrassed to admit this, but we've spent too much time complaining about Product in our Sales meetings. Plenty of griping without talking to the product team directly."

"Not that we've made communication easy though," Tom said.

"Well, yeah, but I know the passive-aggressive emails aren't helpful—especially when we copy other VPs to add pressure and make sure they can see how hard we're trying."

"Ha! The dirty email power play." Tom laughed. "We hate that!"

The two of them were staring at the collusion diagram that was staring back at them.

Ana laughed. "Seeing this so starkly, I'm not surprised that you would see us as impatient, unrealistic, and…what was it you said yesterday?"

"Greedy," Tom said, grinning.

"Right, greedy!" Ana said. "And everything we've been doing just reinforces all of that."

As Ana spoke, Theo finished filling out the diagram.

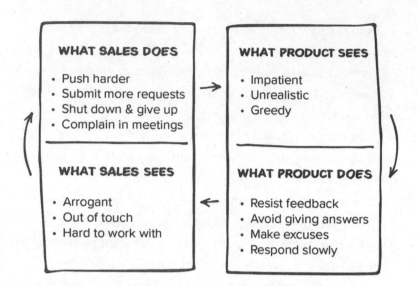

"I'm sorry I haven't come to talk to you about this, Tom," Ana continued. "I should have modeled more straightforward communication for my team."

"Well, we'd like to think we know exactly what we're doing in Product, but I think we actually are too far removed from the customer and your team to be truly effective," Tom admitted. "I haven't helped my people be as curious as we need to be."

"Your team has made some impressive strides," Ana said. "And I think we could really revolutionize things for our clients if we worked better together."

"Maybe we can ask for help to comb through and combine some of the product change requests to reduce redundancy," Tom said. "That would help us respond more quickly."

Theo had taken his seat while they were talking to each other, and only now did Ana and Tom notice. What Tom and Ana had seen—the diagnosis—was already doing its work.

"Look at the board," Theo said, smiling. "Finally recognizing how the inward ways you have been seeing each other drives the problematic behavior that you thought was justified—that's enough to discover a better way."

Lou clapped his hands. "The future looks bright, Theo. Don't you think?"

25 · TURNING OUTWARD

"Why was that so easy?" Ana asked. "I can't imagine us having that conversation yesterday. I mean, we could have tried, but I think it would have made things worse."

"You both deserve credit for the work you've done to see each other more clearly," Theo said. "That's what makes it possible to escape collusion."

"I've been impressed with the questions Ana has been asking," Tom said. "They've been really insightful. She's—" He turned to Ana. "*You're* sharp. I can see why you're the Sales lead."

"We can see why she's the Sales lead too," Kate said, walking into the room.

"Kate!" Lou exclaimed.

"It's good to see you, my friend," Kate said, embracing Lou. "And it sounds like I made it in time for the grand finale!"

She looked at the collusion diagrams on the whiteboard. "Y'all have been busy!"

"It's been…" Ana started, then turned to Tom.

"One unusual leadership training," Tom finished.

"And we've really only gotten started," Theo said. "This isn't just an exercise. There's not an exam for you to pass. The only way it makes any positive difference at all is if these concepts are lived. We'll keep working on implementation in our monthly coaching sessions."

"But I think you're off to a great start," Lou said.

"We want to make sure you leave feeling better equipped to see and lead your teams," Kate said. "What other questions do you both still have?"

"I could use help finding concrete ways to put things into practice," Tom said.

"We've tried to structure our company in a way that supports an outward way of working at all levels," Kate said. "We'll give you specific tools to help you lead your teams in an outward way. And it's important that you understand how our reporting practices, incentive structures, and policies are all designed to help people take others into account."

"But ultimately," Theo noted, "it all boils down to helping individuals see and respond to the people around them, so there are some elements that can't be prescribed. The change has to come from you. It'll take some practice to figure it out."

Tom nodded.

"I'm wondering how to pass this information on to others, "Ana said. "I want to talk about it with my husband, but I'm not really sure where to go after 'You have a problem, but you can't see that you have a problem, and your resistance to the idea that you have a problem indicates that you do in fact have a problem.'"

Lou laughed. "You should've heard my conversation with Kate the first time I tried to explain self-deception!"

"It was all over the place." Kate smiled. "But I hadn't ever seen Lou so sincere before. It was like interacting with a new person."

"I'm glad you gave me a second chance," Lou said.

"To answer your question on the work front, Ana," Theo said, "we've been working on a modified version of this training to offer all employees, not just leaders. In the past, we've relied on a sort of trickle-down approach, but we know that sustained cultural transformation requires a widespread shift in mindset in addition to committed and capable leadership."

"I'd love to pilot that with my team!" Ana said. "We could even do something with Sales and Product together. What do you think, Tom?"

"That could be a game-changer," Tom said.

"And when it comes to explaining self-deception at home," Theo smiled, "I bet Lou has an idea or two."

"Helping people understand what you've been learning is important," Lou said. "That's why we've invested this time with both of you. But living it is even more important. As you share what you've learned, remember that we can try to 'teach' and that will just be a way to blame others with a new vocabulary."

"We all exist in relationship," Theo said. "We are who we are in relation to others, and they are who they are in relation to us, at least to some degree. So we can influence the dynamic between us."

"Not that we can force others to change," Kate noted, "or that all relationships are on equal footing. Power differences exist."

"That's very true." Lou nodded. "And still, I am a part of each interaction I ever have with another person." He gestured to the whiteboard. "A collusion cycle can be changed at multiple points by either party. We don't need to wait for others to change before we see their humanity. We can offer them a different, outward version of us to interact with, one that isn't objectifying or blaming. And that can change the entire dynamic.

"Though it doesn't mean things will change immediately. When Cory was in treatment, I started seeing him as a person, really for the first time. When I saw him that way, I wanted to talk to him, but I couldn't. So I started sending him letters. I wrote of happy memories we had shared, asked questions about his experiences, and apologized for ways I had treated him poorly. I wrote to him in the way I should have been talking to him if I had been seeing him clearly.

"He didn't respond at first. But reaching out that way still felt better to me than my anger and blame. And eventually, as the weeks passed, he slowly began to open up. I discovered the boy I never knew I had. He was full of insights and hopes and struggles. He was finally a real person to me, one I had overlooked and assumed I understood. Our relationship transformed because we found a way to see each other again."

"That's beautiful," Ana said. "I want to experience that."

"It looks to me like you have," Kate said. "Things feel very different between you and Tom than they did yesterday morning."

"One of the best parts of my job," Theo said, "is seeing relationships change for the better. I'm excited to see what you and your teams accomplish together."

"I hope you see what it could mean for the people you lead if you are free of self-deception," Lou said, "because when people have an outward mindset and are alive and responsive to one another, there's not much they can't accomplish. That's the great secret behind Zagrum's success. So don't tell anyone." He winked.

Ana was thinking about all that had happened over the last two days as she hurried back to her office. As she walked, she checked Cheryl's calendar—the employee whom Lou had invited her to talk to. Cheryl's schedule was open, and Ana knew that she had to act fast; otherwise, she would talk herself out of it.

"Cheryl, do you have a minute?" Ana asked, noticing the five or six people who were working nearby in the open office space.

"Of course, Ana. How can I help?"

"I've been meaning to talk to you about something. Let's just duck into the conference room."

"Am I in trouble?" Cheryl asked with a half-nervous laugh.

"No, no. But you've been on my mind. Have a seat." The door of the glass conference room closed behind them as they sat down, the corner of the table between them.

"First off, I wanted to talk to you about your presentation last week. I just want you to know that it was excellent. Really excellent. Thank you for your preparation and effort. It was the highlight of the meeting and incredibly helpful to the team."

"Wow. Thank you," Cheryl said, clearly relieved. "I'm glad you thought it went well."

"It did. And I have to tell you, Cheryl," Ana continued, "I was a little surprised that the presentation went so well because I haven't been very helpful to you since I arrived."

Cheryl's eyes widened, but she didn't respond.

"I didn't invite you to meetings that you should have been a part of, and I haven't done a good job generally keeping you in the loop. I'm sure that's had a negative impact on you. I'm really sorry."

"Thanks, Ana. I appreciate that. I've just assumed that you were busy and learning the ropes about who is doing what, but I did start to worry that maybe I had upset you or that you weren't happy with my work."

Ana's gut clenched. *I should say something about her performance*, she thought. But she found herself saying, "Not at all. I'm sorry I gave you that impression. Anyway, I'll let you get back to it. Thanks, Cheryl."

As Ana walked back to her office, the relief she wanted to feel was clouded.

She sat down to answer some emails, but she couldn't process anything she was reading.

Lou's words from earlier that day sat heavy in her mind:

"Not wanting to be mean or confrontational seems like a positive motivation. But leaders have an obligation to help others improve. Shirking it is neither helpful nor kind."

The conversation we just had wasn't about Cheryl, Ana thought, finally surrendering to the truth. *That was about me wanting to feel better about having misjudged her. But I didn't tell her the truth about my earlier concerns. I stopped short.*

Just then the sound of the desk clock seemed louder than Ana remembered. Tick. Tick. Tick.

But I didn't really stop short, right? Ana thought. *I took responsibility. And taking responsibility is the main thing.* The justifications were coming fast now. *Cheryl pulled it together with that presentation, and bringing up anything before that would just be deflating. I need to keep her motivated, and I did apologize, and—*

The pattern was so predictable that Ana almost didn't see it.

But her exchange with Theo kept running in the back of her mind:

"I don't think they're getting the real me," she had said.

"And consequently, you might not be getting the real them," Theo had answered.

She thought about what Tom had said about the conversation he had with Kate and what Theo had shared about Lou:

"Having an outward mindset doesn't mean overlooking others' shortcomings. Lou didn't let me off the hook for dropping my assignment, but he also didn't reduce me to being my mistake. I was inspired to be better because Lou and I both knew I could be."

Tick. Tick.

It's all justification! Ana thought, shocked by her own honesty. *I have to be real. I have to tell Cheryl the truth. She matters like I matter. If I were her, I'd want to know.*

As Ana almost ran back to the other end of the third floor, she noticed the clock on the wall. It was now past five o'clock, and Cheryl's desk was empty.

Running past the elevator, Ana took the stairs two at a time.

"Cheryl, wait!"

Cheryl's hands were on the door.

"Oh! Hi, Ana."

"I'm so glad you're still here. Do you have a few minutes? There's something else."

"Okay, sure," Cheryl said, sounding wary.

The lobby was empty, and Ana and Cheryl moved to a set of secluded chairs. "I want to talk to you about the conversation upstairs," Ana began as they sat down across from each other. "You mentioned worrying that I hadn't been happy with your work, and I wasn't fully transparent. I don't have the easiest time offering feedback, but I'm working on being more straightforward.

"The truth is, I *had* been worried and even frustrated about some aspects of your performance. You seemed disengaged to me or maybe not giving all that you could. But I didn't talk to you about it, even though I should have. Then your presentation really showed your strengths, and I could see you are incredibly talented. And I wasn't sure why I hadn't seen that before. What's it felt like for you, Cheryl? Do you feel like you were giving 100 percent before the presentation?"

Cheryl inhaled deeply.

"Look," Ana said, "this is weird, I know. This is not how I normally talk to people. And I know that answering honestly might even feel dangerous because you don't really know me. I haven't let you get to know me. But I want you to succeed, and I think I can help, but only if it feels like it's safe to be honest with each other."

"You're right," Cheryl said, finally relaxing. "This is weird!"

Their shared laugh was a first between them.

"And," Cheryl continued, "it's hard not to feel defensive. But I'm actually grateful you're asking. I don't think I've had a manager talk to me like this before. Actually, I was feeling worried after the merger. Things felt uncertain, and I was feeling burned out and then nervous when you joined. I think I just wanted to fly under the radar for a while, but then, ironically, I felt bothered that no one seemed to care if I was here or not. But I thought I would throw myself into that presentation just to see if anyone noticed."

"Well, we noticed!" Ana said, smiling. "Thank you for telling me."

"So now what?" Cheryl asked.

"We can't afford to have that less engaged, less committed version of you on the team. But we *need* that other version of you, Cheryl. We need you to bring whatever version of Cheryl showed up to deliver that presentation. She's the person we need on our team. And I'm ready to help her. Can you do that?"

"Yes, I can do that. I'm actually really excited to do that," Cheryl said.

"Well, let's find time next week to sit down and get really clear on what the team needs from you moving forward and how I can help."

"Perfect. Thanks for this, Ana."

At that moment the elevator opened, and Tom walked out into the lobby.

"Tom!" Ana said, standing. "Cheryl, do you know Tom Callum?"

"Great to meet you," Tom said, shaking Cheryl's hand.

"You're new, right? In Product?" Cheryl said, slinging her bag over her shoulder.

"That's right," Tom said.

"Well, welcome to Zagrum! See you next week, Ana."

27 • MOVING FORWARD

"What an interesting couple of days!" Ana said as she and Tom walked out into the parking lot.

"Really different than what I was expecting," Tom said. "How are you feeling about it all?"

"It's going to take some time to process," Ana said. "But I think it feels like a better way to try and show up. I've been caring too much about being liked and then avoiding some uncomfortable but important conversations. What about you?"

"It seems so obvious, but I didn't realize how often I'm oblivious to the way I'm impacting other people." Tom shook his head, then paused. "Actually, I've been feeling like I should ask you what it's been like to work with me and how I could have a better impact."

Ana took a breath and hesitated. She had expected talking to Cheryl to be the hard part of her day.

"But we can talk another time too," Tom said, second-guessing his timing.

"No time like the present, right?" she replied, and Tom mirrored her smile. "It hasn't been a walk in the park, but some of that is because of my own self-doubt and wanting to be seen in certain ways. I had heard about how well you know the industry, and I was worried I'd look inexperienced or ignorant, especially when I learned it would just be you and me in this training with Theo."

Tom nodded and kept listening.

"I've noticed you can be quick to dismiss ideas sometimes," Ana said, "maybe especially when they're coming from me or my sales team, and that can shut down people's willingness to collaborate. I don't think you should stop seeing potential concerns or weaknesses, but sometimes your certainty and delivery send the message that you're the only one with the right answer, and everyone else is slow. Does that make sense?"

"Yeah, I can see that," Tom admitted. "I can definitely do better at listening longer and focusing on the positive aspects of people's ideas. Though, I guess that won't be enough unless I've got the right mindset too."

After a moment, he added, "I've spent a long time being the kind of leader who tries to have all the answers and tells people what to do. That's even been my approach to parenting. But I don't think it's been working so well."

"Seems like it might be hardest to apply all this outside of work," Ana said, thinking about the recent tensions with her husband. "Which is probably where it matters most."

"Well, we definitely get a lot of opportunities to practice," Tom said. "My weekend homework is having an outward mindset toward a moody teenager."

"Good luck with that." Ana smiled.

"I'll take it," Tom replied. "And maybe you and I can meet on Monday to keep brainstorming ways our teams can work better together. I think they need opportunities to meet and see each other differently and also to understand how our goals are interconnected."

"Good ideas," Ana said. "There's no way our teams will start collaborating if we don't lead this way. You and I could organize a call with everyone and present the collusion diagram to show how we've all been contributing to the challenges."

"That's sounds like a good plan. I'm sure it would help a lot."

"Great. Well, see you on Monday, Tom."

As Tom got into his car, his phone buzzed with a text from his daughter, Becca: "Can we still go to a movie tonight?"

He smiled and responded, "Definitely. You choose! I'll be home soon."

Ana called her husband, Jaime, and heard laughter in the background when he picked up. "Another water fight?" she asked with a smile.

"Guilty," he replied. "We got hot jumping on the trampoline, and one thing led to another. Summer flies by so fast, so I thought it wouldn't hurt. The kids and I made some pizza too. They're excited for you to try it. Should be ready to eat right when you get home."

"Sounds perfect. Tell them I'm on my way, and I'm picking up ice cream."

RESOURCES FOR READERS

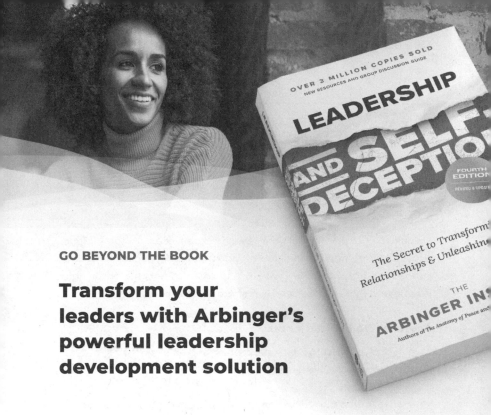

GO BEYOND THE BOOK

Transform your leaders with Arbinger's powerful leadership development solution

A leader's mindset drives what they do and their impact on the people they lead.

For this reason, leadership development that does not address mindset cannot equip leaders with the ability to sustainably transform their teams. Arbinger's solutions uniquely help leaders reconsider how they lead and equips them with the tools required to enable a fundamental shift from the self-focus of an inward mindset to the people-centric, results-focus of an outward mindset.

Without fail, leaders who leverage an outward mindset bring out the best in others and build highly engaged and productive teams.

Learn more at:
arbinger.com/outward-leadership

JOIN THE ARBINGER BOOK CLUB

Unlock the full potential of your reading experience with the Arbinger Book Club. Arbinger's book club provides the perfect space to explore, connect, and grow with fellow book enthusiasts. Engage in meaningful discussions, share insights, and learn from fellow readers.

Access a Wealth of Resources

Gain exclusive access to additional content and practical tools to put into practice what you've learned in the book.

Dive deeper with our discussion guide crafted to enhance your understanding of the ideas presented in this book as well as additional materials, videos, and group activities that invite further exploration and application of the concepts presented.

GROUP DISCUSSION GUIDE

To assist you in processing the ideas in this book and applying them in real and practical ways, we have created a group discussion guide. We have included in the following pages the group discussion guide for part 1 of this book. You can access the full discussion guide and additional content and tools online at **arbinger.com/leadership-and-self-deception**.

In this guide, you will encounter helpful summaries of the main ideas, group processing questions and activities, and ideas for further exploration and application. Even if you are not reading this book as part of a group, the resources in this guide are equally powerful when used individually.

For readers who are serious about joining the thousands of clients who have successfully applied these ideas to their organizations to achieve lasting cultural transformation, this guide provides a helpful primer to prepare you to participate in Arbinger's initial training that launches each transformation process.

Additionally, readers of this book can become certified to deliver Arbinger's transformative workshops within their organization and participate as a catalyst for the dramatic transformations Arbinger helps its clients achieve.

CHAPTERS 1, 2, and 3:

STUCK IN THE DEEPER PROBLEM

Core Ideas

Theo is meeting with Tom and Ana to help them see a problem that they have but can't see—the problem of self-deception. To illustrate this type of challenge, Theo shares an experience he had working on a deal in San Francisco as a young corporate attorney. Reflecting on his experience, Theo asks, "How could I be utterly convinced I was dedicated and self-sacrificing in San Francisco when everyone else on the project could see that I was distracted and disengaged? We sometimes cause or amplify our own challenges but seem to be completely unaware that we are doing so."

Of course, self-deception is not just a lack of awareness that we are causing problems. If the issue were only a lack of awareness, becoming aware would be enough. But self-deception is also characterized by resistance to the possibility that we are causing these problems.

Group Processing

In your reading group, try to identify experiences of self-deception by recognizing times when you believed you were doing your best given the circumstances but, upon more honest reflection, you were actually just finding excuses in your circumstances for not doing your best.

_____

_____

If someone had suggested at the time that you were not doing your best, how would you have responded, and why? What does that reveal about the nature of self-deception?

_____

_____

CHAPTER 4:

THE WORK OF A LEADER

Core Ideas

The most important work of a leader is to see clearly and to help others see clearly.

Group Processing

Describe the best leaders you have ever had. What made them so effective? How did they see you? How did they help you see those you were meant to lead, work with, and serve?

_____

_____

Further Exploration and Application

Having discussed the work of a leader, Theo helps Tom and Ana surface the distorted ways their teams see the other team. He explains to them that, more than any of the unproductive behaviors they are engaging in, the bigger problem is "the way your teams are seeing each other, and the fact that each of them believes that their perception is the truth." Why? Because the perception the teams have of each other shapes every interaction between them.

Seeing this dynamic between the two teams, think of groups you are aware of or a part of who are engaged in conflict. How are the ways they are seeing each other leading to their unproductive or destructive behaviors? How will the ways these groups see each other keep them from discovering solutions?

_____

_____

CHAPTERS 5 AND 6:

DEATH, DENIAL, AND A DISEASE OF PERCEPTION

Core Ideas

The Semmelweis story serves as an important metaphor to understand the nature of the disease that is self-deception. In the story, the physicians who were trying to heal patients were the very ones spreading the disease. Like childbed fever, the disease of self-deception is a sickness that infects our perception. It has a disastrous impact on relationships. And it is highly, dangerously contagious.

The carriers suffer from what is medically called *anosognosia*—the inability to recognize their own illness. The Semmelweis story, Theo says, "is a stark warning. If we don't see clearly, we may harm the very people we intend to help."

Group Processing

Why did the physicians in Vienna General Hospital resist the discoveries Semmelweis made and the procedures Semmelweis recommended even though human lives were at stake?

_____

_____

When have you made matters worse because you didn't see a situation correctly? What were the consequences? And how did you finally come to see that you were part of the problem?

_____

Further Exploration and Application

As Theo revisits his experience in San Francisco, he reflects on how he had lost sight of the fact that his job wasn't only to fulfill his obligations, it was to fulfill them in a way that enabled others to succeed. "Each of us is interconnected to other people," he says, "so there's no way our performance can be accurately measured without accounting for the impact we have on others. To be a parent, or a coworker, or a leader is to be in relationship with real people—people we significantly impact. But that's exactly what I fail to see when I'm self-deceived and have an inward mindset. In fact, it's the very thing I don't want to see. When I'm inward, I only see the negative ways that others impact me."

With this in mind, consider your roles, professional or personal, and list them below.

MY ROLES

1.

2.

3.

4.

5.

6.

Who do you impact in the way you do your work? Who is depending on you? What are their objectives, needs, hopes, and desires?

Who I Impact	Their objectives, needs, hopes, and desires

As you consider these questions, who do you need to learn more about to ensure your efforts are having the right impact? What could you do today to improve your impact?

_____

_____

_____

_____

_____

_____

_____

CHAPTERS 7 AND 8:

THE ROOT CAUSE AND ITS SYMPTOMS

Core Ideas

When we see other people as people, we have impressions, ideas, or senses regarding how we can be helpful to them. Disregarding these senses is an act of self-betrayal—a failure to act on or honor the senses we have toward others when we are seeing them as people.

Group Processing

Identify a time when you had a sense regarding what you should do to respond to another person but you failed to honor that sense. Fill out your own self-betrayal diagram below and include a description of how you saw yourself and the person you had felt called to respond to.

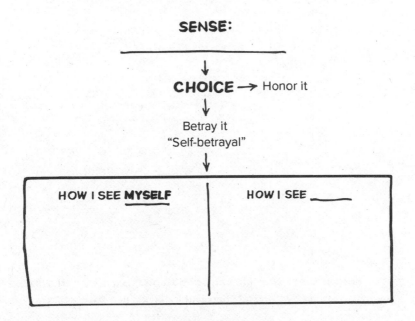

SENSE:

↓

CHOICE → Honor it

↓

Betray it
"Self-betrayal"

↓

HOW I SEE **MYSELF**	HOW I SEE _____

Now ask yourself the following questions and share your discoveries with your discussion group or a trusted advisor:

- Did you see yourself as better than or worse than the other person?

- How were these ways of seeing yourself and the other person distortions of reality?

- Have these inward, self-deceived ways of seeing yourself and others become chronic?

- Do you notice this false self-image showing up in other situations or interactions?

- What is it like to live and work with you when you see yourself and others in these ways?

_____

_____

_____

_____

_____

_____

_____

_____

_____

Visit **arbinger.com/leadership-and-self-deception** to access the full group discussion guide and additional Arbinger resources and tools.

RESEARCH ABOUT SELF-DECEPTION IN ORGANIZATIONS

Self-deception is the most debilitating of organizational issues. This is because problems can't be solved if the people responsible for the problems remain resistant to the possibility that they may need to change.

We share an example of this issue in our book *The Outward Mindset*, an exploration of multiple case studies that illustrate how to turn teams and organizations outward. The story is particularly relevant as it is about the man who was the inspiration for Lou in *Leadership and Self-Deception*. His name was Jack Hauck.

Jack was the founder and longtime CEO of a company called Tubular Steel, a Saint Louis–based national distributor of steel and carbon products. Years ago, Jack had engaged one of the world's best-known consultants to help Tubular overcome the toxic infighting that plagued the senior management team and stymied the growth of the entire company. After months of trying one approach after another without success, Jack asked this consultant if he knew of any other approach the company could try. The consultant was acquainted with Arbinger's work and recommended that Jack explore our ideas.

During our first meeting with Jack and his team, we focused on helping each executive team member reassess their contribution to the challenges the company faced by carefully considering the following statement: As far as I am concerned, the problem is me.

Jack was eager to solve his company's problems, and he saw real promise in this approach. However, he remained blind to how he was failing to apply our work to himself. At the end of the first day with his team, feeling energized by the headway he thought they were making, he stood up to reaffirm his commitment to the effort. "I want you all to get the message," he said. "I'm going to have posters made and put up all over the building." Then, pointing his finger at the assembled executives and officers, he said, "Don't forget: as far as you are concerned, the problem is you!"

You can imagine the reaction of his team members. In the very moment Jack thought he had gotten the point, he had completely missed it. This blindness to personal responsibility is the problem of self-deception. Gradually, Jack overcame this blindness and began to see more clearly. As a result, his company completely turned around, even in the face of a difficult economy in which the market for its products was collapsing. Over a three-year period, the market size for Tubular Steel's products shrunk from ten million tons to six million tons, but the company tripled its revenue over that same period. Tubular Steel was able to achieve this growth only because the team members were able to evaluate, quantify, and address the problem of self-deception that had been holding them back.

Arbinger Research about How to Assess Self-Deception

Our research has revealed a way to assess the level of self-deception in an organization. Participants in our workshops anonymously rate their own and their organizations' mindsets on a continuum from 0 to 10—from *entirely inward* to *entirely outward*. Interestingly, on average, people rate themselves much higher on this continuum—that is, as much more outward—than they rate their organizations. As you might expect, this result surprises no one. People nearly universally expect that they and others will rate themselves more highly than they will rate their organization. Why is this so universal? How is it that, almost without exception, every single employee of an organization believes that they are personally more outward than the collective of employees that make up the organization as a whole?

The math, of course, doesn't work. A company that truly deserves a rating of 4 out of 10 on the mindset continuum, for example, can't be populated by people who, on average, rate themselves at an 8 on the same continuum. The difference between how we rate ourselves and how we rate others is what we call the *self-deception gap*. Self-deception is what explains this often overinflated view of ourselves relative to others.

Our research shows that people intuitively know of the problem of self-deception. They know of it not primarily because they recognize it in themselves but because they observe in others the tendency to overinflate performance relative to results, and they observe how people explain this difference by blaming others for problems rather than taking responsibility. An interesting aspect of self-deception is that people who observe and recognize these behaviors in others are no less likely to engage in the same problematic, counterproductive behaviors themselves. However, they believe their own self-assessments are more accurate than the overinflated, self-congratulatory assessments of their peers. Just like Jack Hauck at Tubular Steel (or Lou Herbert), they see the problem—they just don't see it in themselves.

Measuring the Self-Deception Gap

This nearly universal self-deception gap is reaffirmed in formal assessments we administer within our client organizations. A survey instrument called the Arbinger Mindset Assessment measures in a detailed way where respondents rate the mindset operative throughout their organization and where they rate their own.

The mindset assessment asks questions that measure characteristics such as awareness, helpfulness, accountability, alignment, collaboration, self-correction, coordination, inclusivity, generosity, transparency, focus on results, openness, appreciation, recognition, empowerment, initiative, engagement, and psychological safety. Looking at these various elements and averaging results across industries, we have found that people rate their colleagues in their organizations at an average of 4.6 on the continuum, whereas they rate themselves on average at 6.8. In other words, individuals rate themselves 40 percent better than the rest of the people in their organizations relative to these characteristics.

The self-deception gap between respondents' self-views as compared to their views of others narrows with respect to one of the characteristics in the mindset assessment. In our experience, this characteristic is the single biggest indicator of mindset in an organization. We call this characteristic *horizontal alignment*, which is a measure of the extent to which people understand the objectives, needs, and challenges of those lateral to them in their organizations.

The reason why horizontal alignment is such a helpful indicator of mindset is that a hyperactive self-interest—which is what drives someone who is inward—doesn't incentivize a person to build awareness about the objectives, needs, and challenges of their lateral coworkers. Self-interest may well drive someone to learn about the objectives, needs, and challenges of their boss, but an inward mindset won't invite the same effort toward people situated horizontally from oneself in an organization. From the perspective of an inward mindset, that kind of effort doesn't seem to be relevant as it seems unlikely to make much of a personal difference. The inward-mindset perspective is wrong on both counts, but the blindness perpetuated by that mindset obscures reality.

Interestingly, people rate their own and their organizations' horizontal alignment lower than any other characteristic in the assessment, regardless of organizational size, sector, or industry. Accordingly, efforts to increase horizontal awareness within and across teams is a key step in eliminating self-deception. To this end, Arbinger equips leaders with practical tools to help them increase the horizontal awareness and alignment that is key to collaboration and reduce the competing objectives and silos that undermine accountability and organizational results.

Accessing and Using Arbinger's Mindset Assessment

The Arbinger Mindset Assessment is available for your use. It is a twenty-question instrument that takes less than five minutes to complete. You will receive an automated analysis of your individual and organization's mindsets based on your answers. You may take the assessment free of charge at **arbinger.com/assessments**.

If you wish to get data on a team, department, or entire organization, Arbinger can grant you access to the group-level instrument, which will yield a group-level assessment that includes, among other data points, a measure of the self-deception gap in the organization. Contact Arbinger to set up a group-level assessment and access the transparency required to enable real change.

INDEX

ABOUT THE ARBINGER INSTITUTE

The Arbinger Institute helps leaders transform their organizations by enabling the fundamental shift in mindset that leads to exceptional results. From developing leaders and building high-performing teams to transforming the culture of entire organizations, Arbinger enables its clients to create the mindset transformation required to achieve lasting change. With over four decades of experience, Arbinger is trusted by organizations around the world and in every industry.

The Arbinger Institute is the author of three best-selling books. *Leadership and Self-Deception*, originally published in 2000, introduced Arbinger's work to a global audience and now ranks as one of the top fifty best-selling leadership books of all time.

The Anatomy of Peace, first published in 2006, is perennially among the top-selling books on conflict resolution worldwide and has been printed in over thirty languages.

The Outward Mindset, first published in 2016, shows how organizations successfully implement the ideas discussed in *Leadership and Self-Deception* and *The Anatomy of Peace*. Individually and together, these books help readers see their lives and work in entirely new ways and discover practical and powerful solutions to the seemingly unsolvable problems that plague organizations.

Worldwide interest in Arbinger's work has propelled the growth of the institute across the globe. Headquartered in the United States, Arbinger has offices throughout the Americas, Europe, Africa, the Middle East, India, Oceania, and Asia.

To learn more about Arbinger's solutions, please visit **arbinger.com**

ALSO BY THE ARBINGER INSTITUTE

THE OUTWARD MINDSET

How to Change Lives and Transform Organizations

"The secret to teamwork is an outward mindset. This is the definitive guide on how to achieve it."
–Steve Young, two-time NFL MVP and Hall-of-Fame quarterback

"These concepts are transformational for any type or size of organization."
–Dave Friedman, Chief of Staff, Office of the CEO, Citrix

"A powerful book with a powerful message about really seeing. It opens a path to trust, collaboration, creativity, and performance."
–Katherine Klein, Professor of Management, Wharton School

With practical clarity, this book describes the one change that can dramatically improve organizational performance, spark innovation, strengthen all your relationships, and make your life and the lives of everyone around you better. The key is to change how you see and relate to the world. Changing from a self-focused inward mindset to an others-inclusive outward mindset makes a dramatic difference in results, satisfaction, and engagement. *The Outward Mindset* presents compelling true stories and simple yet profound guidance and tools to help individuals, teams, and organizations move from the stagnation that is a hallmark of the inward mindset to the outward way of working that enables exceptional results.

"Leaders who serve others with an outward mindset encourage a culture of collaboration where everybody wins. Read *The Outward Mindset* and learn how great servant leaders think."

—Ken Blanchard, coauthor of *The New One Minute Manager*®

Paperback, 192 pages, ISBN 9781523087303
PDF ebook ISBN 9781523087310
800.929.2929

Berrett-Koehler Publishers, Inc.
bkconnection.com

Berrett–Koehler
Publishers

Berrett-Koehler is an independent publisher dedicated to an ambitious mission: *Connecting people and ideas to create a world that works for all.*

Our publications span many formats, including print, digital, audio, and video. We also offer online resources, training, and gatherings. And we will continue expanding our products and services to advance our mission.

We believe that the solutions to the world's problems will come from all of us, working at all levels: in our society, in our organizations, and in our own lives. Our publications and resources offer pathways to creating a more just, equitable, and sustainable society. They help people make their organizations more humane, democratic, diverse, and effective (and we don't think there's any contradiction there). And they guide people in creating positive change in their own lives and aligning their personal practices with their aspirations for a better world.

And we strive to practice what we preach through what we call "The BK Way." At the core of this approach is *stewardship,* a deep sense of responsibility to administer the company for the benefit of all of our stakeholder groups, including authors, customers, employees, investors, service providers, sales partners, and the communities and environment around us. Everything we do is built around stewardship and our other core values of *quality, partnership, inclusion,* and *sustainability.*

This is why Berrett-Koehler is the first book publishing company to be both a B Corporation (a rigorous certification) and a benefit corporation (a for-profit legal status), which together require us to adhere to the highest standards for corporate, social, and environmental performance. And it is why we have instituted many pioneering practices (which you can learn about at www.bkconnection.com), including the Berrett-Koehler Constitution, the Bill of Rights and Responsibilities for BK Authors, and our unique Author Days.

We are grateful to our readers, authors, and other friends who are supporting our mission. We ask you to share with us examples of how BK publications and resources are making a difference in your lives, organizations, and communities at www.bkconnection.com/impact.

Dear reader,

Thank you for picking up this book and welcome to the worldwide BK community! You're joining a special group of people who have come together to create positive change in their lives, organizations, and communities.

What's BK all about?

Our mission is to connect people and ideas to create a world that works for all.

Why? Our communities, organizations, and lives get bogged down by old paradigms of self-interest, exclusion, hierarchy, and privilege. But we believe that can change. That's why we seek the leading experts on these challenges—and share their actionable ideas with you.

A welcome gift

To help you get started, we'd like to offer you a **free copy** of one of our bestselling ebooks:

www.bkconnection.com/welcome

When you claim your **free ebook**, you'll also be subscribed to our blog.

Our freshest insights

Access the best new tools and ideas for leaders at all levels on our blog at ideas.bkconnection.com.

Sincerely,

Your friends at Berrett-Koehler